UNLOCKING
the
SECRETS
of the
SHROUD

UNLOCKING *the* SECRETS *of the* SHROUD

Gilbert R. Lavoie, M.D.

ThomasMore®
– *An RCL Company* –

Allen, Texas

ACKNOWLEDGMENTS

Photos used within text are used with permission and copyright protection of Holy Shroud Guild, Esopus, N.Y.; copyright 1978, Vernon Miller; and Gilbert Lavoie.

Holy Shroud Guild: pages 18; 19; 20; 21; 22; 23; 24; 25; 26; 27; 39; 80; 81; 98, Figures 6, 7; 103; 122; 128, Figure 1; 129, Figure 1; 130, Figure 4; 131; 133, Figures 11A, 11B; 135; 136, Figure 1; 137, Figure 1; 139; 187; 188; 193; 219

Vernon Miller: pages cover; 15; 35; 53; 54; 55; 57

Gilbert Lavoie: pages 82; 83; 84; 91; 93; 94; 95; 96; 98, Figure 8; 105; 106; 108; 110; 128, Figure 2; 129, Figure 3; 130, Figure 5; 132; 133, Figures 9, 10; 134; 136, Figures 15A, 15B; 137, Figures 16A, 16B; 189; 190; 192

All scriptural quotations in text, unless otherwise noted, are from the *New Oxford Annotated Bible,* copyright 1991.

Quotes from the *Jerusalem Bible,* copyright 1966 by Darton, Longman & Todd, Ltd., and Doubleday and Company, Inc., are found on pages: 7, 97, 146, 156, 179, and 183 (John).

Video on the shroud available from Thomas More®:
Product # 7907   ISBN 0–88347–907–9

Send all inquiries to:

Thomas More®
An RCL Company
200 East Bethany Drive
Allen, Texas 75002-3804

Toll Free: 800–264–0368
Fax: 800–688–8356

Printed in the United States of America

ISBN 0–88347–395–X

1 2 3 4 5   02 01 00 99 98

Contents

"Salvation comes from the Jews."

John 4:22

Foreword

—⁂·—·⁂—

After spending the last 20 years in search of truth, finding myself living on the fine line between Christianity and Judaism, I am now compelled to share with you this story, a story that belongs to all of us. The story delves into the life of one of the principal players of Jerusalem's history—Jesus of Nazareth. Specifically, it deals with a cloth that some believe to be the burial cloth of Jesus. The cloth is called the Shroud of Turin, so named because of the long period of time that it has resided in Turin, Italy.

In 1978, I began to study this shroud. Each year thereafter brought forth more objective evidence demonstrating that this cloth represented an inherently coherent event. However, in 1988, the carbon-dating tests showed that the cloth was not made during the life of Jesus, but sometime between 1260 and 1390.

Why continue to pursue a subject that has been shown by carbon-dating tests to be a 14th-century event? Please join me on a medical and scriptural search that has been my privilege to experience over these past 20 years. Let me share with you why I was compelled to continue to study the shroud in spite of carbon dating. Then decide for yourself exactly what the Shroud of Turin is and whether it has any meaning for you today. Our focus will be on three areas: (1) the Pentateuch and the Prophets, the foundation of Judaism; (2) the last days of Jesus, the corner-stone of Christianity; and (3) the Shroud of Turin, the cloth that may link these faiths as one.

This adventure would never have occurred if it were not for the earlier efforts of the French surgeon Dr. Pierre Barbet. Even though I never met the man, I have felt that he was my mentor. Furthermore, without the generosity of the Italian-born priest Reverend Peter Rinaldi, S.D.B., my wife Bonnie and I would not have had the opportunity to have a firsthand experience in participating in the events of the Shroud Exposition in Turin in 1978, a crucial starting point in becoming students of the shroud. Moreover, this present work would not have been possible without the previous historical, scientific, and scriptural accomplishments from many people from all parts of the world.

I appreciate the editorial efforts and participation of Dorothy Crispino, editor and historian; Dr. Alan Adler, chemistry professor; Read Albright, English professor; Jack Ballas, engineer; Anthony M. Opisso, M.D., scriptural and rabbinical scholar; Kevin Moran, optical engineer; also my patient family, my agent Joyce Farrell, my publisher John Sprague, managing editor Debra Hampton, and all who were instrumental in producing this book, including Becky Ivey and Dee Ready. I am also most appreciative to Vernon Miller, one of the official scientific photographers of the 1978 examination of the shroud, for allowing me to use his photo-graphs. I am grateful to Reverend Frederick Brinkmann, C.Ss.R., for his permission to use the Holy Shroud Guild's 1931 official Enrie photographs. I am especially grateful to the rabbis who instructed me. I also want to thank Jan S. van den Bosch of Dutch Television for his enthusiastic commitment to produce a fine video on this book. Most of all, I want to express my thanks to Reverend Walter Abbott, S.J., theologian, who has guided me over these last several years. He is truly the ambassador of this book.

DOCTOR BARBET: PHYSICIAN DETECTIVE

Chapter One

1961

It was in the spring of 1961, during my first year of college, when I entered an old bookstore in Boston's Scollay Square. Today that bookstore is gone and Scollay Square is now the location of Boston's Government Center. However, the event that occurred on that day was the beginning of an adventure in understanding that continues to move my very being. There at the back of the store was a brown paperback book called *A Doctor at Calvary* by Dr. Pierre Barbet,[1] a French surgeon. As I was a premed student at the time, the title word *Doctor* caught my attention.

I thought that I had purchased a physician's retrospective analysis of the crucifixion of Jesus of Nazareth, but as I began to read Barbet's book, I found that he was dealing with an entirely different subject. His work centered on a cloth that displayed the blood-marked image of a naked man. This linen cloth, approximately three and a half by fourteen feet, is known as the Shroud of Turin.

As I continued to read, I found that this shroud has been kept at Turin Cathedral, Italy, since 1578. It was first introduced into western European history in the 1350s at Lirey, France, by a French knight, Geoffrey de Charny, who never revealed the circumstances of how he obtained this cloth. In 1453, the de Charny family transferred the shroud to the House of Savoy, who

owned it into the 20th century.[2] While in the hands of the
Savoys, the shroud was first kept in Chambery, France, before it
was finally brought to Turin in 1578. However, more interesting
than its recent history is that from the time of its introduction
into Lirey, France, a controversy has raged as to whether or not
this shroud image is the work of a 14th-century artist.[3]

What stimulated Barbet's interest in this cloth was the full-
scale image of the back and front of a man's body. Most
important to the surgeon, Barbet, were the blood marks that
accompanied this image. These blood marks suggested that the
body of a crucified man had been placed in the supine position
on one end of the shroud and then covered by the other end of
this long cloth (Figure 1—A, B, C, and D). Barbet, along with a
number of other students of this linen, believed that it was the
burial shroud of Jesus.

What intrigued these men and what hooked me into the
pursuit of this study was that there was something very unusual
about the photographs of this cloth. Barbet studied the official
photos of the shroud taken in 1931, which are known as the Enrie
photographs. However, as I later learned, the first official photographs of the shroud were taken in 1898 by Secondo Pia, an Italian
lawyer and amateur photographer. It was during the development
of Pia's photographs, in the quiet of his darkroom, that he saw
something on his negative plate that not only astounded him, but
changed forever the understanding of the shroud image. The image
on the photographic negative plate was not the negative image
that he expected. Rather, it was the positive image of a man
(Figure 2—A, B, C, and D). Realizing that his negative plate held
the positive image of a man brought him to another realization:
the shroud image is a negative (Figure 1—A, B, C, and D).[4] How
and why would a 14th-century artist paint a negative image?

Dr. Barbet had his first direct experience with the shroud
during the Turin exposition in 1933. He was on the steps of the
cathedral, and with the help of the light of day, he saw the following:

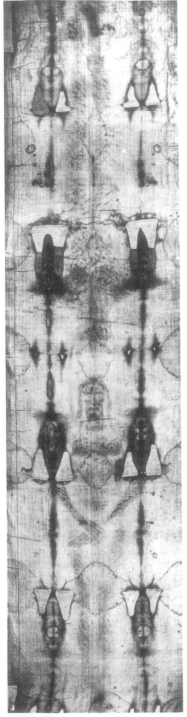 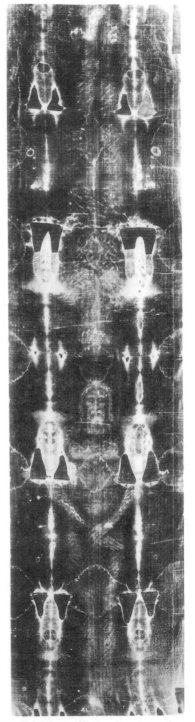

Figure 1A: The actual shroud
is a negative image

Figure 2A: The negative plate
is a positive image

. . . from a distance of less than a yard, and I suddenly experienced one of the most powerful emotions of my life. For, without expecting it, I saw that all the images of the wounds were of a colour quite different from that of the rest of the body; and this colour was that of dried blood which had sunk into the stuff. There was thus more than the brown stains on the shroud reproducing the outline of a corpse.

The blood itself had coloured the stuff by direct contact, and that is why the images of the wounds are positive while all of the rest is negative.[5]

After reading this, I looked again at the photographs, and it was true. The blood was positive on the cloth while the image was negative (Figure 1—A, B, C, and D). In contrast, the blood was negative on the photographic negative of the cloth while the image was positive (Figure 2—A, B, C, and D). This meant that the blood marks were photographically opposite to the image that they accompanied. What pictures carry with them photographic opposites? Other than the shroud, I knew of none.

According to Barbet's eyewitness report, the blood marks were encrusted and intertwined with the fibers of the cloth. As per Barbet, "The blood itself had coloured the stuff by direct contact."[6] It was his experience with wounds and bandages as a surgeon that led him to conclude that the blood marks on the shroud were not what people had been casually calling blood flows, but were actual imprints of blood clots on cloth.

After blood flows from a wound, the blood coagulates and becomes a red, jellylike, moist clot that adheres to skin. A slip of the razor or a careless move with a kitchen knife has caused all of us to experience a bleed that turned into a clot. Barbet recognized that the bloodstains on the shroud were the results of cloth coming into contact with clotted blood. He recognized this as easily as I would recognize the transfer of ink to paper caused by the stamp of a postmaster.

In contrast to the blood marks, the fibers of the image of the man were devoid of anything but the brownish fibers themselves. In the words of Barbet:

> *There is not a trace of painting to be seen, even in Enrie's highly enlarged direct photographs. (To make this clear, one should explain that this is not just a matter of enlarging a photograph, but of an apparatus which produces on the plate an image enlarged seven times, such as a magnifying glass of the same power would supply to the eye.)*[7]

Unfortunately, Barbet did not include Enrie's magnified picture in his book. In order to begin to grasp what caused the image, I had to depend on Barbet's powers of observation and his ability to describe what he saw. All that I knew was that he had not seen paint, but only the "brown stains"[8] that made up the image. I did not understand what those "brown stains" were, but neither did he.

As I turned the pages of Barbet's book, I began to see the subtle details of the image and the blood marks in a way that I would never have anticipated without his medical insights. His observations of the face, especially the swelling under the right* eye, caused me to stop and pay closer attention to the details (Figures 1D and 2D). At first I did not see the swelling, but after comparing the area under the left eye with that of the right, I could see what Barbet was referring to. It was as if the man had been struck in the face with a fist or a stick at the area of the cheekbone.[9]

---

* When speaking of right and left, Barbet is referring to the right and left of the man he believes had been under the cloth.

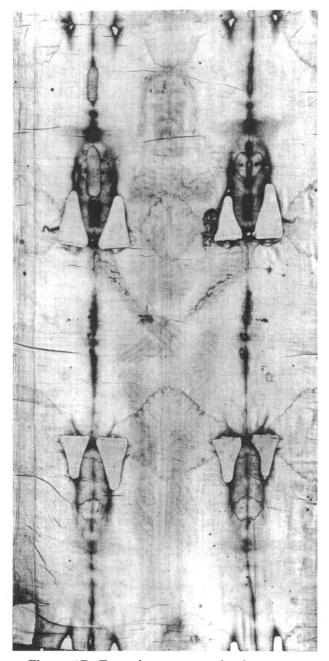

Figure 1B: Front image, negative image

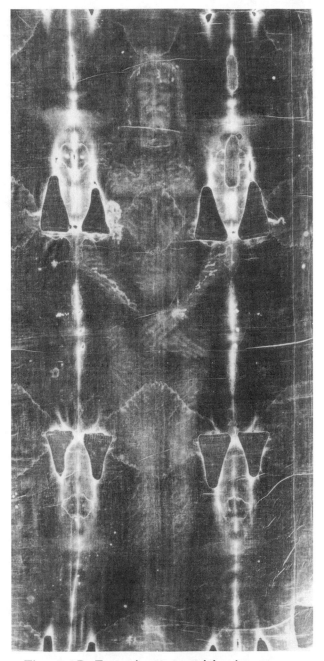

Figure 2B: Front image, positive image

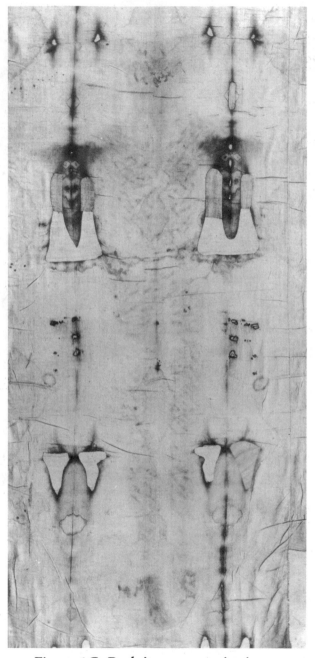

Figure 1C: Back image, negative image

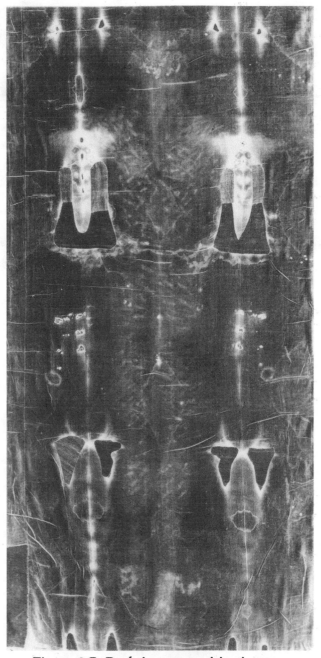

Figure 2C: Back image, positive image

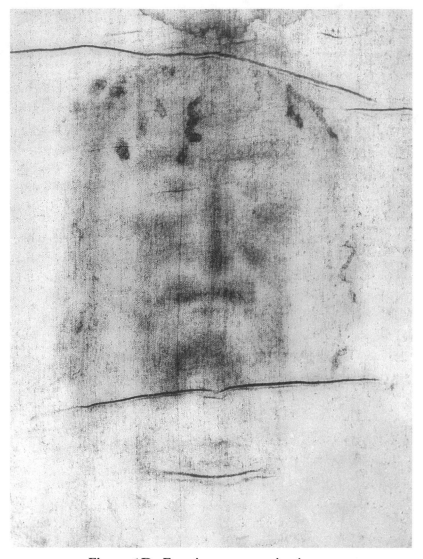

Figure 1D: Face image, negative image

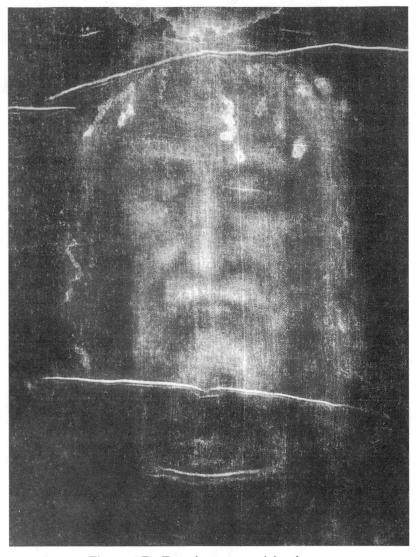

Figure 2D: Face image, positive image

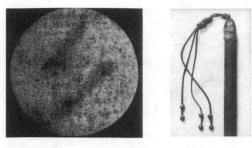

Figure 3

Pair of dumbbell
scourge marks
and flagrum

Just as revealing as his observations of the face was his study
of the scourge marks. These wounds are all over the body but are
best seen on the back image (Figures 1C and 2C). The wounds are
in pairs and are dumbbell in shape (Figure 3). In Barbet's words:
"The two circles represent the balls of lead, while the line joining
them is the mark of the thong."[10] Barbet found that most of these
wounds are in parallel pairs. From this observation, Barbet
deduced that the instrument of scourging had two thongs.
Incredibly, these marks appear to correspond to the design of a
first-century Roman flagrum. The flagrum was made of a handle
from which extended two or more long leather straps that held
bone or lead on their ends. The bone or lead ends were dumbbell
in shape and were designed to pick out the flesh from the victim.

But there was more. Barbet had come to understand something that was even more telling than the details of the individual
scourge marks. His interpretation of the location of these scourge
marks on the body image caught my attention. After reading his
description, I was able to confirm their position. The stripes on
the back image are oblique, slanting upward toward the right and
left shoulders (Figures 1C and 2C). On the buttocks, they change
position and are no longer oblique; they are horizontal. On the
legs, they are again oblique, slanting downward toward the left.
Like Barbet, I contemplated these scourge marks, and I envi-
sioned two floggers, one on each side, standing slightly behind the
victim.[11] They would have alternately flogged their victim at
shoulder height, causing the oblique stripes of the back. Then

Figure 4

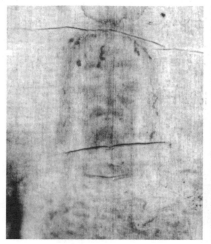 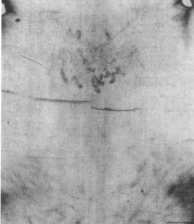

Blood marks	Blood marks
at the face and hair	at the back of the head

they would have struck at waist level, causing the horizontal stripes of the lower backside. Finally, the soldiers would have taken downward swings toward the legs, causing the lower oblique leg wounds. Each strike of small bones on flesh would tear the skin, and blood would flow. Later, these open wounds would ooze clear body fluid like the scraped knees of my boyhood. These injuries would remain moist for hours and eventually allow for the transfer of their paired shapes from body to cloth. There are over one hundred of these marks on the man of the shroud.

Barbet made a study of all the major blood marks seen on the shroud. He discussed the cap of thorns causing the blood flows at the back of the head, face, and hair (Figure 4).[12] He then discussed the side wound of the chest and gave his medical interpretation of the blood flow seen at this wound (Figure 5).[13] By simple observation, I could see that these blood flows followed the force of gravity if one assumed that the body of the man of the shroud had been in the vertical position of crucifixion.

Figure 5

Figure 6

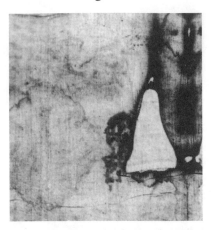

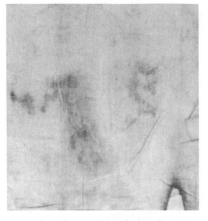

Side wound of the chest   Blood marks of the feet

Barbet also described the blood marks of the feet, which are slightly crossed. Most interesting, however, were his details of the impression in blood made by the sole of the right foot (Figure 6).[14] Finally, he discussed the horizontal blood flow at the small of the back (Figure 7). This blood flow would have meant little to me without his interpretation. According to Barbet, this blood flow occurred after the man was taken from the vertical position of crucifixion and placed in the horizontal position in preparation for burial.[15]

All these studies interested me, but there was one that did much more than that. It was his work on the left wrist and hand

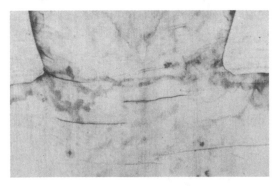

Figure 7

Blood flow
at the small
of the back

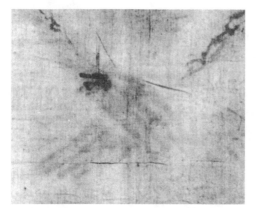

Figure 8

**Image
of the hands
and blood flow
at the wrist**

that remained with me over the years. Even today I marvel at the insights that it brings to the understanding of the shroud (Figure 8). Barbet reasoned that the blood flow of the wrist flowed vertically, "following the laws of gravity."[16] From the vertical flow of this blood mark, he calculated the position of the forearm to be sixty-five degrees from the vertical. In more simple terms, the graphics of this blood mark confirm that the forearm of the man of the shroud had previously been in the position of crucifixion (Figure 9).

Figure 9

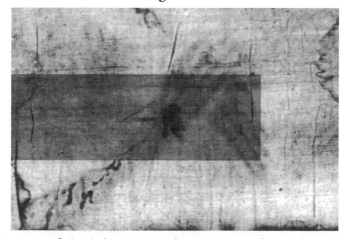

**Image of the left wrist in the position of crucifixion;
shadowed area simulates the crossbeam**

Furthermore, for centuries people believed that those crucified had nails placed through the palms of their hands when being secured to the cross. Prior to the 15th and 16th centuries almost all art forms placed the nails through the palms of the hands.[17] Using cadavers, Barbet demonstrated that the weight of a man cannot be held up if the nails are placed through the palms of the hands. Because of the weight of the body, the nails tear through the flesh and the ligamentous structures of the hands. Barbet demonstrated that to hold a body in the position of crucifixion the nails had to be placed through the bony and ligamentous structures of the wrists. Therefore, the shroud image, with its wrist wound, is anatomically correct.[18]

Intrigued by the wrist wound, Barbet went on to do another experiment. In his own words:

> But these experiments had yet another surprise in store for me. I have stressed the point that I was operating on hands which still had life in them immediately after the amputation of the arm. Now, I observed on the first occasion, and regularly from then onwards, that at the moment when the nail went through the soft anterior parts [of the wrist], the palm being upwards, the thumb would bend sharply and would be exactly facing the palm by the contraction of the thenar muscles, while the four fingers bent very slightly.[19]
>
> The contraction of these thenar muscles, which were still living like their motor nerve, could easily be explained by the mechanical stimulation of the median nerve. . . . And that is why, on the shroud, the two hands when seen from behind only show four fingers and why the two thumbs are hidden in the palms. Could a forger have imagined this?[20]

I looked at the hands of the shroud (Figure 8) and saw for myself that there were no thumbs.

As I finished Barbet's book, his question—"Could a forger have imagined this?"—kept coming back to me. The logical approach that Barbet took, bringing to light the details of the blood marks, the facial beating, the scourging, the crucifixion, and the previously unanswered reason for hands without thumbs, held my attention. Barbet himself did not know the reason for hands without thumbs until he plunged a nail through the wrist of a freshly amputated arm. How could a 14th-century artist have been so anatomically precise, and moreover, why would he attempt to be so precise? Was the artist anticipating the scrutiny of a 20th-century surgeon? Furthermore, this artist would have had to create a negative image five hundred years before the invention of the camera. Then he would have had to put the image on cloth without the use of paint. For me, it seemed that the technology that would have to be attributed to a forger reached far beyond the realm of genius. At the time, from the perspective of a first-year college student, I felt that Barbet had presented convincing medical evidence demonstrating that this cloth once held the body of a man that had been both scourged and crucified. His book left me wanting to know more.

TURIN: BECOMING PARTICIPANTS

Chapter Two

———— ❧ •❀• ❧ ————

1978

In 1978, while reading the *Boston Globe,* I found myself looking at a familiar face that stirred an old memory. Within a moment it all came back to me as clear as it had been on the day that I turned the last page of Barbet's book. I read the newspaper article that accompanied the picture and found that the Shroud of Turin was to be exhibited in Turin, Italy, in the late summer and early fall of 1978.

In late September, 1978, my wife, Bonnie, and I arrived in Turin. We had one purpose in mind: to learn as much as we could about the shroud. However, as our plane landed, I knew that we had no more assurance of succeeding in our venture than would a tourist. In truth, we were outsiders. Furthermore, we were no more experienced regarding the shroud than would be any intent reader of Barbet's book. We were looking for answers, but we did not even know what the right questions were.

After registering at our hotel, we went directly to Turin Cathedral where the shroud was being displayed. We were not alone. In front of us was a line that stretched around a city block. Three million people had come to Turin over those forty days of the exhibition to see the cloth. After waiting three hours, we finally entered the cathedral and could see, displayed by bright lights and under bulletproof glass, the linen cloth that had brought us to Europe. Gradually we made our way up toward the front of the church to about 25 feet away from the cloth. From that position, we could easily see the burn marks and repair patches that parallel the faint yellow-brown image of the front and back of a man (Figure 1). The burn marks were the result of a fire that took place in 1532 at the Holy Chapel of Chambery, in France, where the cloth had been previously preserved. The fire caused some of the silver chest to melt, and molten metal burned through the folded cloth that lay within. The melted silver caused the parallel burn marks that enclose the body image of the cloth. Water was used to douse the flames, saving the cloth, but leaving water rings all along the image area of the cloth (Figure 1).[1] As I looked at the cloth, I found that I was close enough to compare the image marks to the blood marks. I could see that the blood was a dark brownish-red color as opposed to the lighter fragile yellow-brown color of the image. At least at first glance, it looked as if Barbet had reported it as it was.

Prior to leaving for Italy, I had tried to contact Reverend Peter Rinaldi, a priest from Port Chester, New York, who was an active organizer of the current shroud exhibition. Unfortunately, I never reached him; he had already left for Turin. However, I did get his Turin address and wrote to him but never received a reply. In Turin, I found that I had misplaced Father Rinaldi's address. Still determined, Bonnie and I began to search for him on the day following our arrival. Fortunately, I had the name of the hotel where the American scientists who had come to study the shroud were staying. We decided to begin our search for our contact at that hotel. I felt very anxious as we walked along the Via Carlo Alberto where the hotel was located, knowing that we were on an uncertain mission, attempting a rendezvous that depended totally on chance.

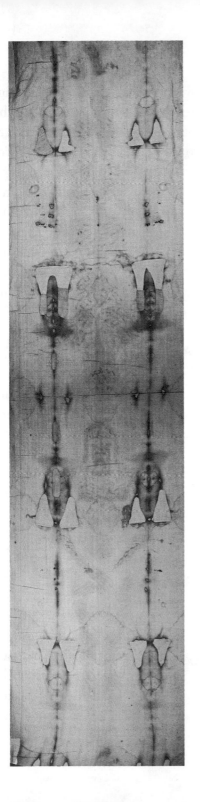

Figure 1

The Shroud of Turin

As we entered Hotel Sitea, we saw several men sitting in one of the alcoves off the lobby. Among them was a white-haired priest. A little embarrassed, we decided that our best strategy was to wait. When the men began to leave, we approached the priest whom we hoped would be Father Rinaldi. I spoke, "Father Rinaldi?" "Yes," he responded. I introduced myself and Bonnie. In a most welcoming tone he said: "My dear Dr. Lavoie, I am so glad to see you!" We were both surprised and moved by his warmth. He acknowledged that he had received my letter. After a short interchange, he assured us of an introduction to some of the members of the American scientific team that had come to study the shroud. He also promised us an opportunity to take close-up pictures of the shroud inside the cathedral. Finally, he gave me one of the last available tickets to the 1978 International Congress on the Shroud of Turin that was to be held the following week. Because of Father Rinaldi's hospitality, we were no longer tourists. Within those few minutes, we became participants in the principal events surrounding the last days of the shroud's exhibition of 1978. Years later I asked him why he treated us with such enthusiasm? His answer, "It was your persistence."

The next day we attempted to learn as much as we could about the shroud. We were told about a small museum dedicated to the history of the shroud on Via San Domenico, not too far from the cathedral. As we entered the museum, Secondo Pia's camera took center stage. It was a large square camera made of wood and was well over two feet in all dimensions. As I looked at it, I realized how large Pia's negative plates had to have been. Because of their size, I had never paid much attention to the small negatives that always accompanied my own photos. However, with Pia's camera in front of me, I could appreciate how he could readily see the details of the positive image of the man of the shroud as it developed on his large negative plate.

Turning from Pia's camera, I began looking along the walls of the small museum. There hung 15th- and 16th-century artistic reproductions of the shroud. These handmade copies demonstrated little similarity to the actual shroud image; they were almost childlike in design. Next, I came to a glass counter. Staring back at me through the glass was the distorted image of a face imprinted on cloth. On further observation I could see that the nose and cheeks of the image were flattened, accounting for much of the distortion. Under the visage was the name Vignon. I recalled Vignon and his theory of image formation in Barbet's book. The masklike face had been produced by placing aloes on a linen, which was then placed over a face prepared with ammonia. The theory was that the ammonia would be derived from the decomposition of body urea (formed by sweat and blood). Barbet, however, felt that Vignon's theory was unsound and even Vignon himself lost confidence in it as the years passed.[2] Nevertheless, I was quite excited about my find and felt that I might be getting closer to understanding the cause of the image. Even as I stood there, I knew that there was a difference between the face on the shroud and the grotesque face behind the glass, but I did not know what caused the difference.

Bonnie and I were intently studying the face when a short round-faced, blue-eyed priest holding a black homburg and displaying a broad smile approached us. "Fellow Americans, I take it," he said, extending his hand to me. It was Reverend Joseph Donovan; we soon became friends. During that trip, Father Donovan bought life-size photographic negative and positive images of the shroud that I later used in my own studies of the cloth. Without his photographs, my story might not have happened.

After we exchanged a few words, Father Donovan invited us to join him. We followed him to an upstairs office above the museum where he was to meet Father Rinaldi with the intent of getting one of the few remaining tickets to the shroud symposium.

As we walked into the office, we met Dorothy Crispino, the secretary, who was also from the United States. She had come to Turin to participate in the organization of the symposium. After the symposium of 1978, Dorothy began to publish a journal, *Shroud Spectrum International,* which gave many the opportunity to have their studies reviewed by others interested in the shroud. Some of the articles that I was able to contribute to her journal became the stepping-stones leading to the completion of this work.

Bonnie took an immediate liking to Dorothy and insisted that she join us for dinner. Before leaving the museum that evening, Dorothy gave us a tour of the small facility. The tour included showing us the life-size positive image of the shroud. The illumination of the shroud image was innovative. The source of light came from behind the photo and shone through the image. While sitting in the darkened room, gazing at the life-size picture of the back image, Dorothy commented, "You know, one thing that this light does is that it brings out the roundness of the muscles, as if the person were right there in front of you." At that moment I agreed, but I did not comprehend the importance of the observation until years later (Figure 2).

On the following day, excited about our discovery and the friends we had made, Bonnie and I decided to head for the Egyptian Museum of Turin. I wanted to confirm that linen cloth could last two thousand years. There we found many fine examples of two-thousand-year-old linens; most were mummy wrappings. Finally, we came across a linen shirt that was in perfect condition, and it was well over two thousand years old. Once I saw that shirt I knew that if linen is kept in a dark, dry place, its longevity is assured.

That night Father Rinaldi called our hotel. He had made arrangements for us to enter the cathedral the next day so that we could take photographs of the shroud. He kept his promise.

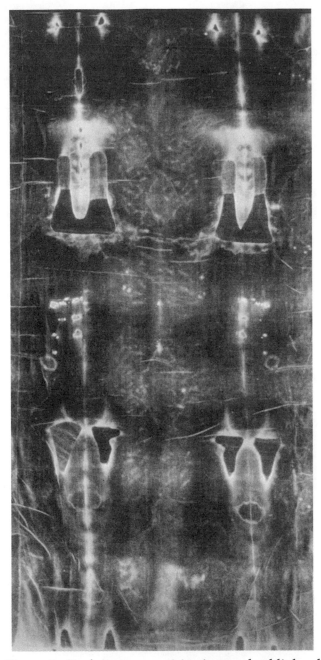

Figure 2: Back image, positive image, backlighted

TURIN:
SCIENCE AND
THE SHROUD

Chapter Three

———— ❦ ··◆·· ❦ ————

1978

Because of the generosity of Reverend Peter Rinaldi, I was now standing on the Piazza San Carlo in front of the Istituto Bancario San Paolo. Inside this structure, the 1978 International Congress on the Shroud of Turin was about to begin. On entering the building, I scanned the conference hall, read through the program, and asked questions, trying to quickly determine who the major players were. Then I let chance do the rest. My first contact was with an older gentleman by the name of Monsieur Antoine Legrand, a man who knew Barbet and studied the shroud with him. I remembered that Barbet had referred to Legrand on several occasions in his book. As Legrand spoke to me, I stood there savoring those few moments that linked me to the past, to an old bookstore in Boston, to the man whose work was the cause of my being there.

Later, as I walked along the central aisle of the auditorium toward the back of the grand room, I met one of the speakers, Dr. Max Frei, a professor of criminology from the University of Zurich. He was a biologist who made a specialty of using microscopic techniques in the field of criminology. He had discovered pollen grains on the shroud and thus was able to give it a geographical history. (Pollen grains are fine powdery microspores that take to the air in order to fertilize their own species.) It had been years since I had looked at pollen under a microscope, and my most recent encounter with it was in the form of a fine yellow-green film that covered my car during the warm season of the year. With Frei standing there in the aisle, I took the opportunity to ask him about his presentation. In fluent English he responded: "It took me five years of my own time to do this work." As he spoke, he pointed to his chest with swift, rapid motions. He spoke with a satisfied smile, and I could sense the enthusiasm that he felt for his work.

In 1982, I read his paper. Here are some excerpts from his study:

> *In 1973, together with two other experts, I was invited by the Archbishop of Turin to compare the structure of the Shroud's tissue, as seen on the photographs taken in 1969, with the original structure of the weave itself. I then discovered under my microscope a certain amount of dust between the linen threads.*

> *I requested and was given the permission to take samples of this dust by means of adhesive tape. . . .*

> *It was a very difficult task to identify the different pollen-grains in the dust collected. First I had to extract them from the sticking-tape and after cleansing they were embedded in glycerin jelly as permanent mountings, so that they could be studied from all sides under the light-microscope. The only true scientific method for identification of pollen-grains is the direct comparison with a mounting in the same medium of ripe pollen collected from a species to which the unknown pollen might belong.*

> *The main problem in this procedure is to find out the right varieties for comparison. Fruitful ideas for comparison often originate from the study of books*

and articles with clear pollen pictures. A good help is the microscopical examination of all pollens available from private collections or public herbariums. In the case of the Shroud, all these sources gave only very few positive results. So I was obliged to make systematic studies of pollen-producing plants growing in such countries where the Shroud— supposing it was authentic—might have been contaminated. A positive identification of such pollens would be a confirmation of the Shroud's stay in that particular botanical region, while negative results concerning the whole flora of a country would allow the exclusion of the geographical area in question as source of contamination.[1]

Frei's words, "confirmation of the Shroud's stay in that particular botanical region," caused me to think of the shroud as a cloth that carried its own passport. Instead of the stamp of the customs' official naming the country of entrance, there were the pollens that clung to the cloth allowing Frei to determine its itinerary. Frei's own words best tell us what he discovered:

From 1974 to 1978, I traveled several times (in different floreal seasons) through Palestine, Turkey (especially Anatolia and the region around Constantinople), through Cyprus, France and Italy, collecting pollens for direct comparison under the microscope. I devoted all my spare time to these journeys and the consequent laboratory work. . . .

I succeeded in identifying 57 different plants which have left microscopical evidence on the Shroud. . . . Every identification has been controlled not only under the optical microscope at magnifications ranging from 60x to 1200x, but also under the scanning electron microscope. . . .

None of the pollens was glued to the cloth with tempera or covered with tempera. This is strong evidence against the possibility of the Shroud's being a painted fake.[2]

Frei found desert plants that grow in soils that have a high concentration of salt. Many of these plants grow around the Dead Sea and are not found at all in Italy and France. He found plants of rocky hills that grow in Israel and neighboring countries. (Two still grow on the walls of ancient Jerusalem.) He found Mediterranean plants that grow in Israel as well as in France and Italy. He found plants from Anatolia as well as some from Constantinople (Istanbul). He found plants that are widely distributed in central Europe (France and Italy). He found no plants from Cyprus.[3] Frei concluded that:

Plants on the Shroud from Palestine and Anatolia are so numerous, compared to the species from Europe, that a casual contamination or a pollen-transport from the Near East by storms in different seasons cannot be responsible for their presence, as I have explained in several conferences and publications. The predominance of these pollens must be the result of the Shroud's stay in such countries where these plants form part of the normal vegetation.[4]

Frei leaves us with two very interesting pieces of information: (1) Even though the known history of the shroud is confined to France and Italy from the 1350s on, with Frei's pollen study we now know that the shroud did have an earlier Asian and Holyland history that preceded the 1350s. This history was either unknown or for some reason never passed on by its first recorded European owner, Geoffrey de Charny. (2) Frei found no tempera on the pollens of the shroud. This was significant in that he took some of his sticking-tape samples directly from the shroud image in 1973. Frei felt that this was strong evidence against the shroud image being a painting. It also confirmed Barbet's personal observations, as well as his deductions from looking at Enrie's magnified picture of the shroud image, that the shroud image was not a painting.

A new dimension has been added to Frie's study through the work of Alan Whanger, M.D., and his wife, Mary. In 1989, while attending a shroud symposium in Paris, the Whangers showed me their observations of very faint images of flora on the non-image areas of the shroud, mainly about the head of the image. They identified 28 species of plants, all found in Israel. In 1995 the Whangers went to Israel seeking the help of Professor Avinoam Danin, an authority on the plant life of Israel, who works at the Alexander Silberman Institute of the Life Sciences at the Hebrew University.

On April 13, 1997, the Department of Media Relations and Publications from the Hebrew University of Jerusalem released a news article and the following excerpts tell the story:

> *Prof. Danin examined their [Whangers'] findings, verified them, and even determined that additional images found on the garment could be associated with plants from the land of Israel. . . . Danin found images of summer and winter leaves of zygophyllum which are characteristic of the plant pollen grains from the rockrose [which] were recovered from the shroud in the 1970's by Dr. Max Frei, a forensic scientific expert from Switzerland. This kind of "double proof" (images and pollen) shows conclusively that there were indeed rockroses that were placed with the shroud, says Prof. Danin.*

> *Prof. Danin says that his research shows that the*
> *types of plants found on the shroud—when*
> *compared to his mapping of these same plants as*
> *found in nature—show that 70 percent of these*
> *species can be found within a 10 x 10-square-*
> *kilometer area whose center lies in an area between*
> *Jerusalem and Jericho. Prof. Danin noted further*
> *that the zygophyllum grows only in Israel, Jordan*
> *and Sinai, with its northernmost boundary in the*
> *world being at the sea level sign on the highway*
> *between Jerusalem and Jericho. In view of this, one*
> *can narrow down even further the origin of the*
> *shroud and say definitely that one is dealing with*
> *the Jerusalem area. The fact that a winter leaf was*
> *found on the zygophyllum, together with remnants*
> *of the stalk from the preceding year, proves, says*
> *Prof. Danin, that it was plucked in the spring,*
> *which was the season identified with most of the*
> *plants revealed on the shroud.*

The Whangers and Professor Danin thus complement Frei's work and present evidence that the shroud originated in the Jerusalem area in the spring of the year which is the time of the Passover. A precedence for using flowers in Jewish burials is found in 2 Chronicles 16:14 (verbal communication with Anthony Opisso, M.D.)

Frei's itinerary of the shroud, as determined by the pollens, also coincided with Ian Wilson's theories as to the whereabouts of the shroud prior to the 1350s. Ian Wilson, a history graduate of Oxford and a journalist, is the author of the book *The Shroud of Turin,* published in 1978. He was also presenting at the conference, which gave me the opportunity to hear about his work firsthand. His book is a compilation of fragmented historical reports that tell of an image-bearing linen cloth that carried the likeness of Jesus. He begins his story in the early part of the first century and takes us from Jerusalem to the ancient city of Edessa, now called Urfa, located in the southeastern part of Turkey. There, an image-bearing cloth was given to the incumbent king, Abgar, where it remained hidden for five centuries. It resurfaced at the same site in A.D. 544 as "the divinely made image not made by the hands of man"[5] as it was reported by the Syrian historian Evagrius (527–600). Regarding the image, Wilson quotes Edward Gibbon's *The Decline and Fall of the Roman Empire:*

> *Before the end of the sixth century these images made without hands . . . were propagated in the camps and cities of the Eastern empire; they were the objects of worship and the instruments of miracles; and in the hour of danger or tumult their venerable presence could revive the hope, rekindle the courage, or repress the fury of the Roman legions. Of these pictures the far greater part, the transcripts of a human pencil, could only pretend to a secondary likeness and improper title; but there were some of higher descent, who derived their resemblance from an immediate contact with the original. . . . The most ambitious aspired from a filial to a fraternal relation with the image of Edessa.[6]*

In A.D. 944, the image of Edessa, also known as the Mandylion, which Wilson believes to be the shroud, arrived in Constantinople where it remained for over 250 years. Wilson's theory is interesting, but he has to contend with the fact that the Mandylion was thought to have been a facial image whereas the shroud displays a total body image. He builds up circumstantial evidence to back his theory. He writes:

*The earliest [evidence], datable to sometime before
1130, is an interpolation in an original eighth-
century sermon by Pope Stephen III. Referring to
the Mandylion, it tells us: "For the very same
mediator between God and man . . ., that he [Jesus]
might in every way satisfy the king [Abgar],
stretched his whole body on a cloth, white as snow,
on which the glorious image of the Lord's face and
the length of his whole body was so divinely trans-
formed that it was sufficient for those who could not
see the Lord bodily in the flesh, to see the transfigu-
ration made on the cloth."[7]*

Wilson's most convincing documentation locates the shroud
in Constantinople. From the pages of the diary of a French crusader
by the name of Robert de Clari, we find the following account:

*There was another of the churches which they called
My Lady St. Mary of Blachernae, where was kept
the sydoine [shroud cloth] in which Our Lord had
been wrapped, which stood up straight every Friday
so that the figure of Our Lord could be plainly seen
there.[8]*

*And no one, either Greek or French, ever knew what
became of this sydoine after the city was taken.[9]*

This was written during the first part of the 1200s after
Constantinople was sacked by the army of the Fourth Crusade.[10]
Wilson believes, as some other scholars do, that this was the time
when the shroud, along with many other treasures of
Constantinople, began its long journey to the West. Eventually,
the shroud appeared in Lirey, France, in the 1350s.[11] For those
interested in further details, Wilson's book is a good start as a
reference.

Wilson's evidence is far from complete in connecting the Mandylion and the shroud as one. However, more important than how he resolves the whereabouts of the shroud before it was introduced into western European history by Geoffrey de Charny are the quotes that he uses to build up the evidence for his case. They carry with them a definite common theme. They tell us (1) that in the East there existed a cloth that carried an image of Jesus and (2) that there was something unusual about this image, so unusual that those who described it believed that it was not a painting, that it was not the work of an artist, that it was "not made by the hands of man."

"Not made by the hands of man" hit home when I first read the words. There is a reason why we do what we do. I must admit that after reading Barbet's work, I was moved to want to know more about the shroud image. The driving force that motivated me was the possibility that the shroud image was not made by human hands. It was that lure that brought Bonnie and me to Turin and to the conference that I was attending.

It was years later before I realized that the Bible was very much concerned with this very same concept: things are made either by human hands or by God. From Deuteronomy I read, "There you will serve other gods made by human hands, objects of wood and stone that neither see, nor hear, nor eat, nor smell" (Deuteronomy 4:28). The corollary is well defined in Hebrews: ". . . then through the greater and perfect tent (not made with hands, that is, not of this creation)" (Hebrews 9:11). The biblical meaning is clear: that which is made by human hands is from man and that which is not made by human hands is from God.

After hearing Wilson's presentation, I met with Dr. John Jackson for about thirty seconds as he raced from the auditorium. Jackson, a physicist, was the energy behind the American move to study the shroud. His presentation was one of the highlights of the congress. He placed a photograph of the shroud image under a VP8 image analyzer. This electronic device is ". . . ideally suited for determining whether a given image contains distance information because it converts image shading into relief."[12] Jackson found that the frontal image of the shroud has a three-dimensional quality.[13] This quality of three dimensionality intrigued a number of scientists who followed this enthusiastic man to Turin. John's drive, along with the efforts of all those who came with him to Turin in 1978, deserves much credit for establishing the American scientific literature that is now available on the shroud.

When I met Vern Miller in the grand room of the congress, I was excited to learn that I was being introduced to one of the official professional photographers for the American scientific team. However, I had no idea where that initial meeting would eventually lead me. A few years later I met with Miller at a Boston waterfront restaurant. He had with him a folder of shroud slides that he and his team had taken while in Turin in 1978. Miller held his hand out over the table, handing me a slide that he explained was a micrograph. He explained that it was taken at 64x magnification. It was taken at the image area of the nose, which happens to be the darkest portion of the entire shroud image.

I held the slide to the light, and I could see exactly what caused the image (Figure 1). For me it was the visual confirmation of what Barbet had seen at one yard away in 1933. There was no paint causing the image; anyone could verify this by simply looking at the slide. I could see that the individual fibers of each thread were yellowed. It was these individual yellowed fibers of each thread, not paint, that caused the image. Subsequently, Miller sent me other micrographs. One of them was taken at the blood area of the chest wound at 32x magnification (Figure 2). In and about the fibers is intertwined debris that

Figure 1

Micrograph taken at the image area of the nose
at 64x magnification

Figure 2

Micrograph taken at the blood area of the chest wound
at 32x magnification

Figure 3

Micrograph taken at the image area of the right eye
at 32x magnification

Barbet had believed to be blood. Included is a final micrograph (Figure 3) for comparison to the blood area. It is also taken at 32x magnification but at the image area of the right eye. Just like the micrograph of the nose image taken at 64x magnification, no debris can be seen here.

With Miller's micrographs in hand, I was convinced that the image was not a painting. I wasn't alone. All of the American scientists who studied the shroud, except one, found that it was not a painting.[14, 15] (The work of one scientist,[16] who believes the shroud to be a painting, was carefully reviewed by the other scientists. After careful evaluation, their conclusion was still the same: the shroud image is not a painting.[17]) However, I did not know what had caused the yellowing of the fibers, and I did not know whether the debris that Barbet believed to be blood was indeed blood. The answers to these two questions—(1) what caused the yellowing of the fibers that caused the image and (2) what was the debris that Barbet believed to be blood—came from a man who did not attend the congress in 1978. Jackson and others had arranged to have some of the sticking-tapes that had been placed over the blood marks and image marks of the shroud given to a man by the name of Dr. Alan Adler. Adler, a professor of chemistry from Western Connecticut State University, is an expert on porphyrins, which are organic chemicals that form part of the structure of red blood cells. Adler analyzed the particles and fibers that adhered to the sticking-tapes.

My first encounter with Adler was in his office at Western Connecticut State University in 1982. As I entered his office, he was sitting at his desk surrounded by walls covered with books from floor to ceiling. We began by discussing his work on the red-orange globules that he found on the sticking-tapes that had been placed over the blood areas of the shroud. He told me of the difficulties that he had faced in removing these particles from the tapes in order to prepare them for chemical analysis. He spent a great deal of time explaining his confirmatory tests for blood.

First, he visually compared the microscopic examination of the shroud blood area to a control: a 300-year-old linen impregnated with twelve-month-old blood. Under the microscope, the fibers and the crystals of both were similar in physical appearance, except the crystals of his control sample were slightly more garnet colored.[18] After this examination, he eventually "established by detection of heme derivatives, bile pigments, and proteins,"[19] the presence of whole blood on the shroud. (Anyone interested in pursuing the chemistry of Adler's blood studies should refer to his excellent journal articles.[20])

As we went on to the next topic, that of the yellowed fibers that caused the image, Adler stopped and said, "You know, one of the best tests they did during those five days of testing in Turin was one of the simplest tests they did." He went on to explain the visual test that the team members performed. They shone a light through the cloth. As the light passed through the cloth, the blood images could be easily seen, but the body image could not be seen (Figure 4). What did this mean?

Figure 4

 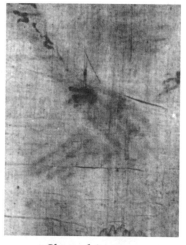

Transmitted light;   Shroud image;
no image seen   normal light

Adler explained that the blood marks were opaque, and because of this, they were poor transmitters of light. In contrast, that which caused the body image was not opaque and was so thin that light went right through it and did not produce an outline of the image as did the blood. This meant that the light went through the image in the same way as it went through the plain cloth. He went on to further support this statement by explaining that the American scientists had removed part of the backing cloth that had been sewn onto the back of the shroud in order to preserve the shroud after the fire of 1532. In doing so, the scientific team discovered that the blood marks had soaked through to the back side of the shroud[21] whereas the image marks were not seen from the back of the cloth.[22]

Adler then explained that a single thread of the shroud cloth was made up of many very small (10 to 15 microns in diameter)[23] linen fibers. The width of one of these fibers is much smaller than that of a human hair. Only the topmost fibers of the thread were yellowed. These yellowed fibers, composed of cellulose, were found only on the image side of the cloth and were responsible for the image. As he spoke, I realized that he was confirming what I had seen for myself when Vern Miller handed me one of his micrographs of the image (Figure 1).

After extensive chemical testing, Adler concluded (1) that there is no paint medium coating the image fibers and (2) that there are no stains or dyes causing the image. Rather, the yellowing of the shroud image fibers was produced by a dehydrative oxidative process that affected the fiber (cellulose) structure itself and caused it to yellow. In other words, this process is a degradation of the fibers themselves and is identical to the aging of linen, causing linen to turn from white to yellow. Adler explained that light, heat, or an acid (such as sulfuric acid) can all yellow linen fibers like those found in the image area of the shroud. Therefore, it was not a painted image, but rather, it was the result of a chemical change of the cellulose itself. (For those interested in the chemistry of the image fibers of the shroud, Adler's article is excellent.[24])

Adler went on to explain that even though he understood the chemistry of the cellulose that makes up the yellowed fibers of the image, he still did not know what event took place to cause the image. He leaned back in his chair and went on to say that with the use of perspiration,[25] the yellowing of the topmost fibers can be reproduced when linen is placed over the flat surfaces of a body. However, when it came to more complex surfaces, such as the face, this contact mechanism is not capable of causing the image that is seen on the shroud.[26] John Jackson spent years attempting to reproduce the shroud image without success. He investigated direct contact, diffusion, radiation from a body shape or an engraving, dabbing powder on a bas-relief, electrostatic imaging, and hot bas-relief (a rubbing image), but none reproduced the image of the shroud.[27] There is presently no known mechanism that can reproduce this body-to-cloth image transfer.[28]

Adler shared with me another piece of information that continues to fascinate me. On removing the blood from the blood-covered fibers, Adler found that these fibers, instead of being yellow as they were at the image areas, were white. What did this mean? Because the fibers under the blood were white, it meant (1) that the blood went onto the cloth before the image marks and (2) that the blood protected the fibers from whatever caused the image to occur. Therefore, the blood came first; the image came later.[29]

I did not meet Dr. Eric Jumper at the congress, but later at the cathedral during a private showing of the shroud. Jumper, in engineering and presently teaching at the University of Notre Dame, spent a great deal of time studying the shroud and published several papers regarding his findings. His best article, "A Comprehensive Examination of the Various Stains and

Images on the Shroud of Turin,"[30] is a must-read for the scientifically inclined. I called Jumper to ask him about the observations
that he had made concerning the image marks. He explained
that their (the scientists') goal was to understand what caused the
image. On viewing the shroud image under magnification
(Figure 1), he and his colleagues found no excess material around
the image fibers. The only place where the fibers were cemented
together was at the blood-mark areas. Furthermore, they found
that the topmost fibers of the threads of the cloth were yellowed,
and it was these yellowed fibers that caused the image.

Jumper followed along the length of the image fibers and
found that as the yellowed uppermost fibers dipped down under
another thread, they were no longer yellow but remained their
original white. Likewise, as the fibers followed a normal twist of
the thread, the top fibers were yellowed while the lower part of
the fibers remained white. Therefore, whatever caused the image
affected only the uppermost fibers, even to the point of not
wicking (absorbing and conveying fluid along a fiber like the
wick of an oil lamp) along the fiber as a liquid would do if it had
been applied to the shroud surface.[31]

As Jumper and his associates teased at the fibers of the threads,
they made another observation. They found that whatever caused
the yellowing of the shroud fibers penetrated down into each
thread the depth of only one fiber. Jumper remembers that after
they left the examining room they argued about whether the
yellowed fibers penetrated the depth of the thread by one or two
fibers. In attempting to decide what was the correct observation,
they all went back to their notebooks to see what they had documented. Everyone had made the same observation: the yellowed
fibers that caused the image were only one fiber deep.[32, 33]

As I listened to Jumper, I felt that I was being taken right
down into the image and fabric of the shroud. I was enjoying
every moment of Jumper's firsthand observations. He was

someone who had been there; he was an eyewitness, just as Barbet had been in 1933. Jumper went on to say that he later looked carefully at the micrographs taken by Vern Miller and made other observations regarding the image fibers (Figure 1). He saw that there were examples everywhere of yellowed image fibers lying side by side to white non-image fibers. He also noted that the yellowing of the individual fibers was uniform: the amount of yellowing of each fiber was a quantitative event. Each fiber that was yellowed was yellowed to the same extent as the next image fiber. In other words, there was no graduating difference in yellowness of the fibers. Rather, each fiber held almost exactly the same quantity of yellowness.

If every topmost fiber of yellowed threads contained the same shade of yellow, then what caused the difference in the shading of the image? Jumper explained that the difference in the shading of yellow from one area of the image to another was dependent on the number of yellowed fibers present. He made a count of them, and if one area was darker than the other, that area would contain more yellowed fibers.[34] Regarding why we see the changes in shading that causes the image, Jumper's words best describe it: "It's like the dots of newspaper print. If you want to make an area darker, you put in more dots."

There is one thing that is certain: the image is not a painting. Jumper is convinced of this and so is anyone who understands his detailed study of the image fibers and also understands the wicking ability of linen. The liquid medium of a paint would wick along the fibers and color the fibers as they dip below the threads of the weave. Furthermore, a liquid medium would spread adjacently from fiber to fiber, and if enough is added, it would soak through to the opposite side of the cloth. If the paint were more viscous (thick), it would collect on and between the fibers. It would not look like what is seen at the image areas, but would look more like what is seen at the blood areas.

Several years ago, I followed up on a claim that the shroud image is a painting and examined the artist's rendition. First of all, the image was not even the same color as that of the shroud image, but more important, the medium had soaked through to the back side of the cloth. That experience has made me realize the significance of Jumper's very specific description of the image fibers of the shroud. Those who claim that the shroud image is a painting will have to demonstrate that their reproduction matches what Jumper and his associates have described at the fiber level of the cloth. At the same time, they will have to create a negative image. The difficulty of producing the shroud image by hand is best underlined by the words of Dr. Adler:

> *For a painter to have created this image, he would have needed a paintbrush the size of a fiber which is less than half the width of a human hair.*

On the last day of the congress, there came an intense cry for carbon dating; it came from every country represented. In response, it was explained that there was a new carbon-dating technique available to date the shroud, and all one needed was a single ten-inch thread. However, no one was to have the opportunity to perform carbon dating for another 10 years.

JEWISH
BURIAL CUSTOMS

Chapter Four

1979

On returning from Turin, I decided that I would study the blood marks of the shroud. However, the question was: How does one begin to study the blood marks on the shroud cloth—blood marks that some claim to be the creation of an artist? It was 1979 when I called Harvard University and asked for the name of a professor who was a specialist in iconography, the study of religious images. I was given the name of Dr. Ernst Kitzinger, who had spent a lifetime studying ancient paintings of Jesus from both the East and the West. I was fortunate to meet with him just before his permanent departure to England where he planned to retire.

I asked Kitzinger the following question: "Can you show me some works of artists who have painted blood marks like the ones that you see on the Shroud of Turin?" His response was: "The Shroud of Turin is unique in art. It doesn't fall into any artistic category. For us, a very small group of experts around the world, we believe that the Shroud of Turin is really the Shroud of Constantinople. You know that the crusaders took many treasures back to Europe during the 13th century, and we believe that the shroud was one of them. As for the blood marks done by artists, there are no paintings that have blood marks like those of the shroud. You are free to look as you please but you won't find any." I did look, and he was right; I have never found any. Nor has anyone else.

If artists had never created blood marks like those of the shroud, then there had to be some explanation as to why the blood marks of the shroud were unique. I decided to go back to the basics and deal with what was at hand—the blood marks of the shroud itself. The only logical option available was to attempt to reproduce the blood marks of the shroud. If Barbet were right and the blood marks were actually transfers of moist clots on a body to cloth, then there should be no problem in reproducing them. However, if I was to pursue this study correctly, I felt obliged to go back into history and find out how the Jews buried their dead at the time of Jesus.

To my surprise, I found that the Jewish burial custom at the time of Jesus was the same as it is today: when a person dies, the body is washed prior to burial.[1, 2] Furthermore, this custom was well known, and Christian scholars had assumed for centuries that Jesus' body was washed because "they took the body of Jesus and wrapped it with the spices in linen cloths, according to the burial custom of the Jews" (John 19:40). However, since there are numerous blood marks on the shroud cloth, it is evident that the man covered by the shroud was not washed. If Jesus had been washed according to the Jewish custom, then one would have to conclude that the Shroud of Turin is not the shroud of Jesus.

Believers in the authenticity of the shroud had a different perspective. Over the past 80 years most of the books written by the proponents of the shroud state that the body should have been washed as part of the Jewish tradition, but it wasn't washed because the Sabbath was imminent, and therefore, there was no time to wash the body. That is the information that I had available at the start of my study. However, when Bonnie and I finished our academic pursuit of how the Jews buried their dead at the time of Jesus, I understood the real meaning of John's words "according to the burial custom of the Jews."

John Reagan, a pharmacist in West Roxbury, Massachusetts, where I practiced medicine, said that he would not have any trouble finding out how the Jews used aloes and myrrh in their burial rites. When I entered his pharmacy weeks later, he greeted me with a smile of accomplishment and said, "I couldn't find anything on aloes and myrrh, but I did find that the Jews don't wash the blood from the body of a man who dies a violent death." I was astonished and blurted out, "Where did you find that?" "In Lamm's book, *The Jewish Way in Death and Mourning.*"

It was just as Reagan said:

> *The blood that flows at the time of death may not be washed away. When there is other blood on the body that flowed during lifetime, from wounds or as a result of an operation, the washing and taharah [purification] are performed in the usual manner.*
>
> *Where the deceased died instantaneously through violence or accident, and his body and garments are completely spattered with blood, no washing or taharah is performed. The body is placed in the casket without the clothes being removed. Only a sheet is wrapped around it, over the clothes. The blood is part of the body and may not be separated from it in death.*
>
> *Where blood flows continually after death, the source of the flow is covered and not washed. The clothes which contain the blood that flowed after death are placed in the casket at the feet.[3]*

Lamm's information was convincing. However, scholarship required that Bonnie and I pursue this back to the time of Jesus.

It was during our search for the source of the ritual of not washing the blood of a man who dies a violent death that my perspective of Christianity and Judaism began to change. It was then that I realized that we could not pursue this subject back to the time of Jesus by pursuing Christianity's historical documents. To do this right, we had to follow the path of the Jewish faith into history.

Bonnie found that Lamm's work basically paraphrases the laws found in the Code of Jewish Law from the 16th century. The following quotes are from the more recent abridged version of the code:

> 9. *If a person falls and dies instantly, if his body was bruised and blood flowed from the wound, and there is apprehension that his life-blood was absorbed in his clothes, he should not be ritually cleansed, but interred in his garments and shoes. He should be wrapped in a sheet, above his garments. That sheet is called sobeb. It is customary to scoop up the earth at the spot where he fell, and if blood happens to be there or near by, all that earth is buried with him. Only the garments which he wore when he fell are buried with him, but if the blood splashed on other garments, or if he was placed upon pillows and sheets while the blood was flowing, all these need not be buried with him, but they must be thoroughly washed until no trace of blood remains, and the water is poured into the grave. If, however, the deceased did not bleed at all, his clothes should be removed, his body cleansed and wrapped in shrouds, as is done in the case of a natural death. . . .*

10. If blood has flown from the injured body, but it stopped and his clothes were removed, after which he recovered and lived for a few days and then died, he must be cleansed and dressed in shrouds. Even if his body is stained with the blood which issued forth from him, he must be cleansed, for the blood lost while being alive is not to be regarded as life-blood; we are only concerned with the blood which one loses while dying, for it is likely that this was his life-blood, or it is possible that life-blood was mixed with it.[4]

There is no doubt that there was an exception to the normal custom of simply washing the dead prior to burial. If death is by violence and blood flows at the time of death, the victim does not undergo the ritual of washing, but the body is simply placed in a sheet and buried. This was true from the present to as far back as the 16th century, but in order to be certain that this ritual took place at the time of Jesus, we had to look further.

Pushing back to the time of Jesus in the New Testament brought forth no definite clues. It was only when I began to read the Pentateuch, the first five books of the Bible, that I began to get some insights regarding God's word to his people concerning blood. It was in Genesis that the first real evidence appeared:

Every moving thing that lives shall be food for you; and just as I gave you the green plants, I give you everything. Only, you shall not eat flesh with its life, that is, its blood.

Genesis 9:3–4

Again, I came across this theme, but expanded, in Leviticus (the third book of the Pentateuch):

If anyone of the house of Israel or of the aliens who
reside among them eats any blood, I will set my face
against that person who eats blood, and will cut
that person off from the people. For the life of the
flesh is in the blood; and I have given it to you for
making atonement for your lives on the altar; for, as
life, it is the blood that makes atonement. Therefore
I have said to the people of Israel: No person among
you shall eat blood, nor shall any alien who resides
among you eat blood.

Leviticus 17:10–12

The books of Genesis and Leviticus helped me to begin to understand why the Jews had a concern for blood. However, not eating blood was a concept totally different from not washing blood from the body of a man who died a violent death. The source of this ritual continued to elude me.

Eighteen months later I was still no closer to the source of the Code of Jewish Law regarding not washing. Finally, through the help of a close friend, I got the names of three academic rabbis. The first two leads were not helpful. I was in my office when I made the third call. I can remember my anticipation as I asked, "Do you know the source of the Jewish custom of not washing the blood from a victim who died from a violent death?"

The rabbi's response was an emphatic "Yes," and he continued talking. "Do you have Danby's English translation of the Mishnah?" I responded, "Yes." He continued, "Well look at Nazir, 7[2] page 289. Also look at Oholoth, 3[5] page 653. Read what it says about blood and mingled blood." He went on to explain that the concern was over the blood that flows at the time of death. With regard to mingled blood, not only was the timing important but the amount of blood was also important. It had to amount to a quarter-log of blood that he defined as the contents of a small wine cup. He went on to say that this blood would be considered unclean. At the time I didn't really understand some of his terminology such as *unclean, quarter-log,* and *mingled blood.* It did not matter, for I now knew that I finally had a documented source of the nonwashing ritual. As I hung up the telephone, I was amazed at his immediate knowledge. I believe that this man knew the entire Mishnah by memory. The words of this scholarly rabbi still resound in my mind. I shall be forever grateful to him.

On arriving home that night, I went to the Mishnah. I found in the introduction a paragraph stating the Mishnah's origin. It read, "The Mishnah may be defined as a deposit of four centuries of Jewish religious and cultural activity in Palestine, beginning at some uncertain date (possibly during the earlier half of the second century B.C.) and ending with the close of the second century A.D."[5] It covered the period of time I was looking for—the life span of Jesus of Nazareth.

I went directly to the first passage that the rabbi had given me in Nazir. It was a list of body parts that rendered one "unclean," unclean as one would be if one touched a corpse.[6] Confused by what I read, I decided to move on to the second quote that the rabbi had given me. As I read the words from the Mishnah, I sensed the age of their composition. The author was qualifying and quantifying and thus defining the blood of a crucified man. I suddenly sensed that these lines of text had been waiting there for centuries, waiting to be rediscovered and understood by our own generation.

> *What counts as 'mingled blood?' If beneath a man that was crucified, whose blood gushes out, there was found a quarter-log of blood, it is unclean; but if beneath a corpse, whose blood drips out, there was found a quarter-log of blood, this is clean. R. Judah says: It is not so, but the blood that gushes out is clean and that which drips out is unclean.*

Note 1. According to one view, in the intermittent dripping of the blood the uncleanness of each drop in turn is nullified by its smallness in quantity; therefore the whole quarter-log is clean. According to the other view the slowness of its dripping is proof that it issued after death, and it is therefore unclean.[7]

It took me a long time to come to grasp the full meaning of these words, but it was all there—the explanation of why the blood of a man who dies a violent death is buried with the body. Mingled blood is the mixture of blood that issues while a man is alive with blood that issues from the man from the moment of death. The blood that issues while a man is alive is not important, but once it mingles with blood that flows from the moment of death it becomes mingled blood. For mingled blood to be considered unclean, it had to reach a certain volume as defined in the Mishnah. For mingled blood to be considered unclean, the quantity of blood had to at least amount to "a quarter-log" of blood. A log of blood is the contents of six eggs.[8] Therefore, a quarter-log is the contents of one and a half eggs. This amount is just enough to fill a small wine cup, exactly as the rabbi had described.

However, in order to comprehend why blood is buried with the body of a man who dies a violent death, I had to understand the biblical meaning of the term *unclean*. The following quote from Numbers, the fourth book of the Pentateuch, helped me to come to that understanding:

> *All who touch a corpse, the body of a human being who has died, and do not purify themselves, defile the tabernacle of the* LORD; *such persons shall be cut off from Israel. Since water for cleansing was not dashed on them, they remain unclean; their uncleanness is still on them.*
>
> *Numbers 19:13*

In other words, all who touch a corpse are rendered unclean (Numbers 19:13). If they do not undergo the ritual of cleansing (Numbers 19:2–9, 17–19), they defile the Holy Place and are cut off from Israel. With this understanding of the biblical meaning of the word *unclean*, I began to realize why the rabbi had referenced the list of body parts in Nazir.

The rabbi's first reference had to do with the first order of uncleanness with regard to a corpse. That meant that all the parts of the body that were listed in that passage of the Mishnah rendered one unclean by all means of contact, as unclean as one would be if one had touched a corpse. In other words, touching a body part was like touching a whole corpse, and it caused one to be unclean. Included in that list of body parts that convey uncleanness was "a half-log of blood."[9] That means that if you touch the blood from a corpse, you are as unclean as you would be if you had touched the corpse itself. Therefore, the blood as well as all the body parts must be buried with the body.

Considering a crucified man, the rabbi's second reference, Oholoth, was very specific. A quarter-log of mingled blood that flows from the body of a crucified person conveys uncleanness, the same uncleanness that the corpse conveys. Therefore, the mingled blood on the corpse of a crucified man must be buried with the body. The body is therefore not washed. *The Code of Jewish Law* makes it clear:

> *He should not be ritually cleansed, but interred in his garments and shoes. He should be wrapped in a sheet, above his garments. That sheet is called sobeb. It is customary to scoop up the earth at the spot where he fell, and if blood happens to be there or near by, all that earth is buried with him.*[10]

What is important about mingled blood is not the blood that comes forth during life but that which comes from a man at the time of death. ". . . for the blood lost while being alive is not to be regarded as life-blood; we are only concerned with the blood which one loses while dying, for it is likely that this was his life-blood, or it is possible that life-blood was mixed with it."[11] What is being described here is the "life-blood" of Genesis and Leviticus.

What is life-blood? I found a note in the Mishnah that defines it: "it is inferred that the blood which issues at the moment of death (which is what the Mishnah means by 'life-blood') is the blood that makes atonement."[12] In defining life-blood, the Mishnah refers to Leviticus 17:11. I reread the words from Leviticus:

> *For the life of the flesh is in the blood; and I have given it to you for making atonement for your lives on the altar; for, as life, it is the blood that makes atonement. Therefore I have said to the people of Israel: No person among you shall eat blood, nor shall any alien who resides among you eat blood.*
> *Leviticus 17:11–12*

I thought about these words as well as the Mishnah's definition of life-blood. I was beginning to understand the words of Genesis and Leviticus. They were the words of God. They were the words of the blood covenant that God established with the human race after the great flood. These words were taken seriously by God's people, the people of Israel, so seriously that the blood of all animals is drained before the flesh is eaten. This tradition lives on to this day among the Jewish people who partake of only kosher meats.

After learning about mingled blood, life-blood, and God's blood covenant with the people of Israel, the Jews, I read the Gospel of John with a different perspective:

*Then Pilate took Jesus and had him flogged. And
the soldiers wove a crown of thorns and put it on his
head.*

John 19:1–2

There they crucified him.

John 19:18

*But when they came to Jesus and saw that he was
already dead, they did not break his legs. Instead,
one of the soldiers pierced his side with a spear, and
at once blood and water came out.*

John 19:33–34

I now realize that John's description of Jesus' death had a
different meaning to first-century Jews. I now understand what
they understood by his description. The man who hung on that
cross had upon him blood that flowed during life, mingled with
blood that flowed at the time of death. Mingled blood. It was
life-blood, the blood that makes atonement. It was unclean and
therefore had to be buried with him.

*They took the body of Jesus and wrapped it with the
spices in linen cloths, according to the burial custom
of the Jews.*

John 19:40

Jesus was buried according to the Jewish custom. The corpse
with its mingled blood was wrapped in "linen cloths" and buried.
Therefore, the shroud with its blood marks is consistent with the
history of how the Jews buried their dead at the time of Jesus.[13]
The search that John Reagan started us on was over.

BLOOD OFF THE LEFT ELBOW

Chapter Five

1983

Now that I knew that the shroud blood marks were a historical possibility, I wanted to see if Barbet's theory of blood transfers to cloth was reproducible. However, before beginning this work, I decided to pursue the study of a blood mark that had always intrigued me: the off-the-body-image blood mark located at the left elbow (Figure 1). What intrigued me was that I did not have an explanation as to how this blood mark got to its off-image position. Barbet had never mentioned it, and I never came across any information about it. In looking for answers, I went to the oldest authority I knew—Reverend Peter Rinaldi. He also was unaware of any existing explanation regarding the origin of this off-image blood mark.

The urge to understand the off-image blood mark caused me to hypothesize several theories regarding its origin, but none could be proven. Finally, one Saturday morning, I again retrieved Father Donovan's full-size shroud images from my front closet. As I stood there, looking down at the off-image blood mark (Figure 2), I wondered what would happen if I placed the cloth over my own body. Would it give me more information? The next moment I was down on the rug with the frontal image over me. Once I was satisfied with the alignment of image to body, I

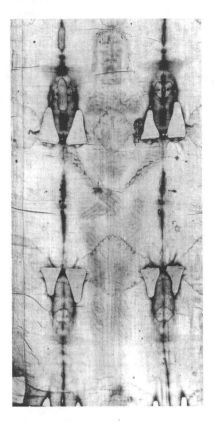

Figure 1

Image of the shroud
with blood mark
off the left elbow*

looked over to see where the off-image blood mark was draping against my body. The location of the drape surprised me. The off-image blood mark was touching the back of my upper arm. I could hardly believe the logical interpretation of what I was seeing. This simple blood mark was leading me in a direction that I had never anticipated.

That same week, the whole family began working on a full-size tracing of the left arm and off-image blood mark (Figure 3). In going through the process of making the tracing, I followed the blood line from the forearm to where it ends its course at the off-image round spot. Never once is the continuity of this line

* The right elbow of the man covered by this cloth.

Figure 2

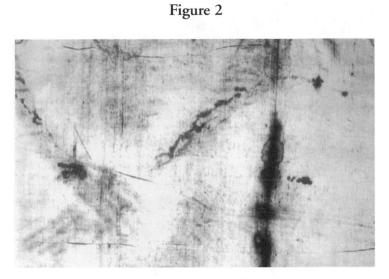

The off-image blood mark

Figure 3

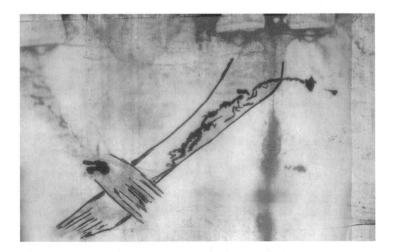

Full-size tracing of the off-image blood mark

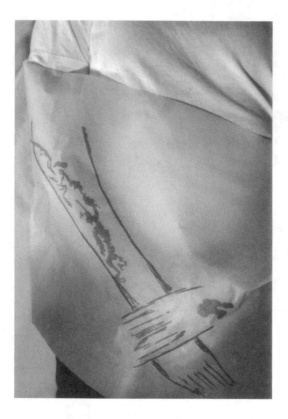

Figure 4

Tracing laid
over a man

broken. Once the tracing was completed, we then turned it over and laid it over one of us in the same way that we felt the shroud cloth had been laid upon a body (Figure 4). From this direct frontal view of the man, I noted that the off-image blood mark was not visible. Furthermore, what I saw through my camera was similar to what I saw on the shroud: an image with no sides. The shroud image is, therefore, similar to a direct frontal photograph of a man.

On the side view of the same subject (Figure 5), the paper tracing drapes over the side of the body, simulating a cloth drape. From this information, it becomes obvious that the off-image blood mark was caused by the cloth touching the clot on the back of the upper arm as the cloth draped over the side of the

Figure 5

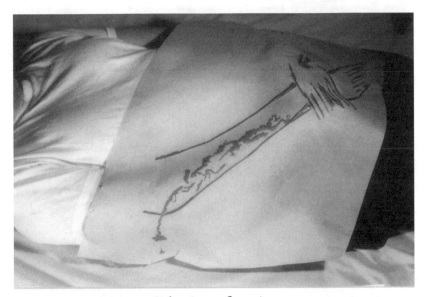

Side view of tracing

body. At this point in the study, I realized that the other blood marks on the image translate into two-dimensional information, corresponding to the man's height and width. However, the off-image blood mark is graphic evidence pointing to yet a third dimension—depth: a three-dimensional figure had been under this cloth.

Finally, we placed the tracing and the arm of the volunteer in the crucifixion position (Figure 6). It was then that the last piece of the puzzle became obvious. The clotted blood on the back of the upper arm represents a prior blood flow that followed the force of gravity. The origin of the blood flow likely started at a wrist wound, which is not visible, and flowed down the forearm, past the elbow, and around the back of the upper arm collecting into a round pool of blood on the underside of the arm. From this pool, I could imagine that excess blood dripped

Figure 6

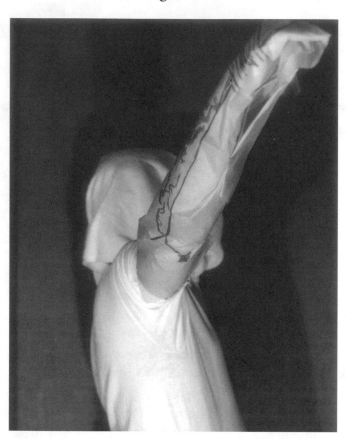

Tracing over a man in the crucified position

off the body onto the ground. It reminded me of the description found in the Mishnah of the blood coming from a crucified man: ". . . but if beneath a corpse [of a crucified man], whose blood drips out, . . ."[1] Indeed, this blood mark is consistent with what was seen at a crucifixion. Furthermore, the path that this blood flow took is real, as real as it is to me every morning after I wet my hand and razor and begin to shave, as real as it would be to any of us who have experienced holding up wet hands while waiting for someone to hand us a towel. In conclusion, the off-image blood mark indicates that the man of the shroud had been in the position of crucifixion. Barbet had made this same observation many years before when he studied another blood mark, that of the wrist. These blood marks of the shroud, therefore, demonstrate a consistent pattern.

The key to this whole study is the force of gravity. The blood had simply followed the pull of gravity, creating an unbroken line that ended in a small, suspended pool of blood. The man was later taken from the vertical position of crucifixion and placed on one end of the long shroud cloth, the other end then having been draped over the body. Again, gravity caused the side of the cloth to simply drape over the side of the victim, allowing the cloth to come into contact with the blood mark on the back of the upper arm. At that point, the shroud cloth touched the moist clot and acted much like a blotter in contact with wet ink: the moist clot left its imprint on the cloth. This blood mark was, therefore, the result of a simple contact process.

Once I understood the process of how the off-image blood mark was formed, I realized that this information brought me to an appreciation of the difference between the making of the blood marks and the formation of the image: (1) The off-image blood mark confirmed that the cloth touched the back of the upper arm. (2) The blood marks of the forearm also confirmed that the cloth had come in contact with the forearm. Therefore, the cloth had skin contact with the back of the upper arm as well as with the forearm. However, there is a major difference between the two. Where the cloth touched the forearm, the image of the forearm can be seen, but where the cloth touched the back of the upper arm, there is no image. Therefore, image formation had nothing to do with the cloth touching skin or sweat products. Why do I say this? Because there is no image on the cloth where the back of the upper arm came in contact with the cloth (Figures 1 and 2). Then what caused the image? I did not know. All I knew was that in contrast to the blood marks, the body image was not created by a contact process. If it had been, an image of the upper arm would be seen extending out as far as the off-image blood mark.

In summary, this off-image blood mark told me three things about the shroud: (1) The shroud cloth had covered the three-dimensional figure of a crucified man. (2) The blood marks were made by a contact process. (3) The image was not made by a contact process.[2]

Even now, when I think about the off-image blood mark, I still sense a certain excitement, for I know that there was a crucified man under this cloth.

THE TRANSFER OF BLOOD CLOTS TO CLOTH

Chapter Six

———— ❦ ·✦· ❦ ————

1983

The off-image blood mark was with me day and night. Understanding the graphics of this blood mark convinced me that the image marks of the shroud were definitely not made by a contact process. Then how did the image get on the cloth? I knew of no scientific explanation, nor could I even contrive any solution. Therefore, I decided to concentrate on the blood marks, something that I felt quite capable of pursuing.

I wanted to confirm what Barbet had inferred, that the blood marks on the shroud were the mirror images of blood clots on skin. In order to make this confirmation, it is important to first understand what Barbet means by "blood clots on skin." Clot formation is the biological reaction that blood undergoes when it leaves the body. (Clot formation also occurs inside the body, but this is not pertinent to our discussion.) Everyone experiences bleeding and clot formation sometime during life: Some form of trauma cuts open the skin, the wound appears, and then the blood begins to flow. Clot formation occurs when the liquid blood changes to a jellylike, solid, red form that no longer flows but sticks to the skin. After the clot is formed, it exudes a small amount of clear yellow serum for a short period of time. Finally, the red, jellylike mass dries and takes on a crusty appearance.

In an attempt to prove that blood clots transfer to cloth, I conceived a simple experiment.[1] First, I placed a thin transparent plastic sheet on a table. I then took fresh blood from a volunteer and immediately transferred it to the plastic surface in the form of eight small pools of blood, using about nine drops of blood to form each pool. I made oblong pools of blood and used the blood mark on the forehead of the shroud image for comparison.

I numbered the pools of blood one through eight. I waited. It took about ten minutes for the liquid blood to clot.[2] After the clots were formed, it took a little over thirty minutes for the eight clots to start clot retraction.[3] (Clot retraction is a biological process whereby the clot actually shrinks in size, and while it does, it exudes or squeezes out a clear yellow fluid called serum.[4]) As the clots were getting slightly smaller, a clear yellow serum was accumulating around the clots. The clot retraction process was occurring to all eight clots at the same time. At this stage, each clot was a red, jellylike, oblong pool surrounded by a clear, pale-yellow halo.

I had also prepared eight small squares of linen cloth to place over these eight blood clots. Exactly thirty minutes from the time that the blood was withdrawn from the volunteer, I covered the first clot with cloth. I covered the second clot thirty minutes later and so on until I had covered each clot in sequential order at half-hour intervals. Four hours from the time that I had drawn the blood, I covered the last clot with a linen square. Twenty-four hours later, I lifted the squares of linen from the plastic surface. A hard, crusted, dry clot covered each cloth. I took a penny and scraped off the excess crusted blood. When I compared the bloodstained cloths to the forehead clot of the shroud, I was both amazed and disappointed at what I saw (Figure 1).

As I looked at the outcome of this simple experiment, I could see that the results of the transfers from clots to cloth were not as neat as the blood mark of the forehead. The forehead clot on the

Figure 1

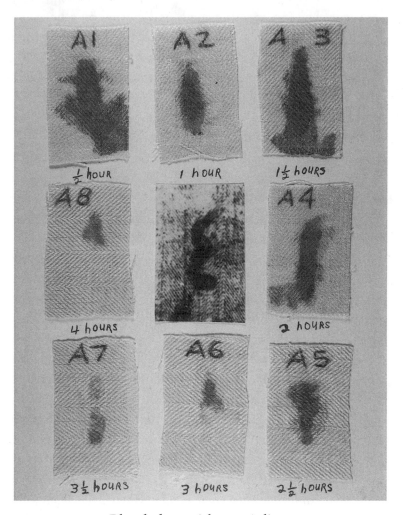

Blood clots with serum lines
Experiment conducted on a horizontal surface

shroud shows what looked like a serum line about the edge, but overall it was more precise than the clot transfers of the experiment. I just sat there at the table looking at the results, wondering why the discrepancy, when suddenly, in the middle of another thought, I realized that I had made a mistake in the design of the experiment. The fact was that the blood clotted on a horizontal surface. The horizontal position allowed the exuded serum to accumulate around the clots and cause an uneven transfer to cloth. But the man of the shroud did not die in the horizontal position; rather, he died in the vertical position of crucifixion, and the blood clotted on his skin while he was still in this position.

I could hardly wait to start the experiment over again. This time, within the first half hour after blood withdrawal, I placed the eight clots in a vertical position. This was time enough to allow for clot formation. As a result, the clots kept their shape and clung to the vertical surface of the plastic surface. After a short time, clot retraction began to occur, and the clear yellow serum was being exuded from the clots. I watched in amazement as the serum dripped down the vertical wall of clear plastic, leaving behind neat, moist, red, jellylike clots. At the same time that I placed the clots in the vertical position, I placed a linen cloth on the first clot. I continued doing this at half-hour intervals until all eight clots were covered, just as I had done with the first experiment. However, the clots no longer collected the pools of excess serum about them as they had in the previous study. After twenty-four hours, I turned the cloths over and found dry, crusted clots (Figure 2). I removed the crust as before. These clot transfers were neat and were more similar to the forehead blood mark (Figure 3). I did a shorter experiment on normal skin, and the results were similar (Figure 4). Therefore, I confirmed Barbet's deduction that some of the shroud blood marks were clots that were transferred to cloth.

As I watched the clot-to-cloth transfers take place, it became obvious that it was the moisture of the remaining serum at the surface of the clots that allowed the transfers to take place. As soon as a cloth was placed over a clot, I would first see the clear

Figure 2

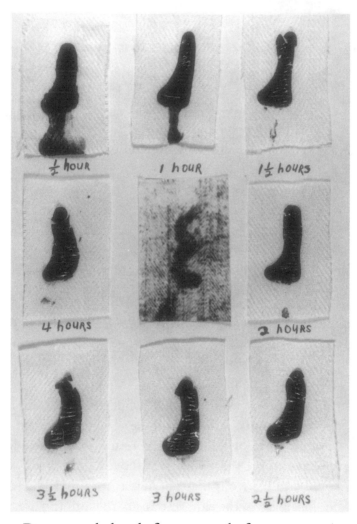

Dry crusted clots before removal of excess crust

yellow serum pass through the cloth giving it a wet appearance. This was followed by the red blood cells of the clot that gave it its final red appearance as the soak-through came to its completion. In the case of the man of the shroud, some of the excess

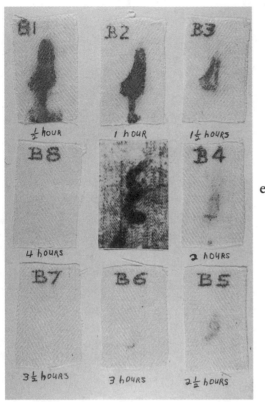

Figure 3

**Blood clots
with
neat clot transfers
to cloth,
experiment conducted
on a vertical surface**

serum dripped away from the clots while the body was in the vertical position. What remained on the skin were neat appearing clots still moistened by the remaining serum, which enabled the clots to seep into the shroud cloth at the time of burial.

I could also see from the experiment that there was a time limit on the ability of the clots to transfer to cloth (Figures 3 and 4). At room temperature, transfers could take place up to one and a half hours after the blood was taken from the volunteer. Over time, as the moisture evaporated from the clot, the clot lost its ability to transfer to cloth. The clot became too dry, and as a result, it could no longer soak into the fibers of the linen. One and a half hours after the time of blood withdrawal, the clot no

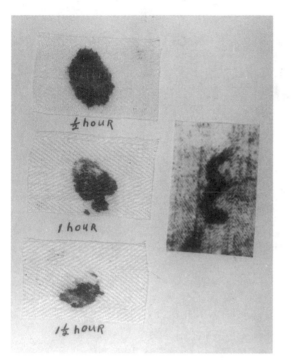

Figure 4

Blood stains transferred from skin

longer made a transfer to cloth (Figures 3 and 4). When the clots are moistened artificially with normal saline, this time can be extended up to two hours (Figure 5).[5] In the case of a crucified man, it may be possible that body sweat could have provided extra moisture.[6]

The experiment of clot transfer to cloth, performed on a plastic surface and normal skin, was not intended to duplicate the actual event, but was done so that this event could be better understood. In doing this experiment, I realized that the ability of the moist clot to transfer to cloth would be affected by many factors, such as temperature, humidity, movement of ambient air, skin moisture, and skin temperature. With regard to the man of the shroud, these are all unknown factors. Furthermore, the timing of the movement of the body from a vertical to the horizontal position could affect the accumulation of serum deposit

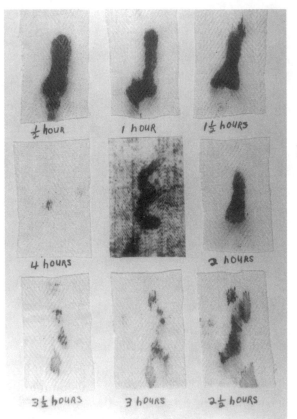

Figure 5

Blood clots
moistened
by normal saline

about the clots and ultimately affect the outcome of clot to cloth transfer. Regardless of all these unknowns, I learned that moist clots, relieved of some, but not all, of their serum by the vertical position of crucifixion, could easily have been transferred to cloth within one and a half hours and possibly up to two hours from the time of the death of the man of the shroud.

What is even more amazing about this timetable is that it corresponds to the gospel account of Jesus' death and burial. The time of death was ". . . three in the afternoon"(Luke 23:44). His burial took place thereafter: "He [Joseph] took it [the body] down, wrapped it in a shroud and put him in a tomb. . . . It was

Preparation Day and the sabbath was imminent" (Luke 23: 53–54, *The Jerusalem Bible*). The time of burial had to take place before the Sabbath because, according to the Mishnah, no part of the body may be moved on the Sabbath.[7] The beginning of the Sabbath was between 5 and 6 P.M. (March and April Sabbath times in Jerusalem).[8]

As I continued to study the subtleties of the shroud's blood marks, I began to realize that the serum from the clots on the man of the shroud did not all drip away as it did on the vertical plastic surface experiment, but rather clung to the skin. For example, in contrast to the neat, barely visible serum lines around the blood mark of the forehead are the more visible serum lines around the blood mark of the wrist (Figures 6 and 7). The location of the wrist wound and its association with the trauma incurred at the wrist explain some of the reasons for the difference.

These serum lines, similar to the serum lines of the first plastic surface experiment (Figure 8), tell another part of the story. Crucifixion, as noted in the Mishnah, was a dynamic, ongoing process of blood dripping or gushing from the crucified. Eventually, the blood on the surface of the body would clot, exude serum, and dry up. But as long as life was maintained, bleeding would continue from the open wounds. All of the serum did not drain away as it did in my simple plastic surface experiment, but some did accumulate on the skin adjacent to the clots. When death finally came, the last blood flows of the wrist clotted and then retracted, and the exuded serum clung to the adjacent skin. The blood mark of the wrist, as seen on the shroud cloth, is the mirror image of that last event. Details like this convinced Barbet, the surgeon, that the blood marks of the shroud represent mirror images of clotted blood. Paint does not separate and create the serum lines that are seen here (Figure 7). Only blood does this.

When I called Vern Miller in 1991 to ask him for some shroud photos, he reminded me of the work he had done in 1978 regarding the blood marks. Using ultraviolet fluorescence photography, he took pictures of the shroud and found that there

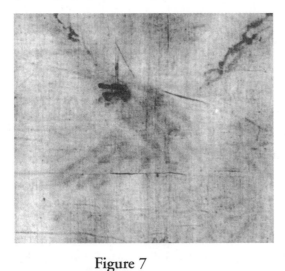

Figure 6

**Blood mark
at the wrist**

Figure 7

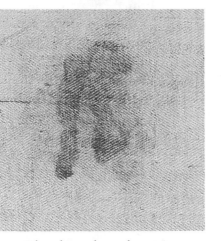

**Blood mark at the wrist
with surrounding serum lines**

Figure 8

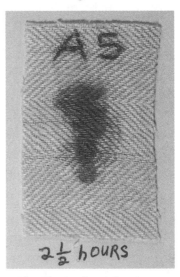

**Blood mark with serum
lines from Figure 1**

were halos of fluorescence around some of the blood marks.[9] For example, there were "clear fluorescing borders around the hand wound blood stains."[10] He went on to say that he was never able to reproduce his findings using blood. In our discussion, I realized that he had not photographed any blood samples with serum lines. In response, I sent Miller the blood marks with serum lines (Figure 1), which were the result of my 1983 transfer experiments. He took pictures of these and found that the blood marks with the serum lines did indeed fluoresce, reproducing the fluorescent halos that he had found around some of the blood marks of the shroud. Because of his persistence in wanting to understand the reason for the fluorescent halos about the shroud blood marks, Vern Miller visually reconfirmed Alan Adler's blood chemistry [11] and my studies as well as the original observations of clot-to-cloth transfers made by Barbet. Indeed, the blood marks of the shroud demonstrate that they had exuded serum.

Having worked in a hospital emergency room, I have had many personal encounters with bleeding patients. People with head injuries tend to bleed profusely because the scalp is very vascular. These patients are usually covered with blood even when the head wound is very small. After examining the numerous blood flows on the head and the face of the man of the shroud, I believe that he must have been completely covered with blood. This blood eventually dried and, therefore, made no transfer to cloth. The only blood clots that transferred to the shroud were those that contained moisture. Those blood clots would have resulted from the last blood flows that occurred near and at the time of death. Therefore, the blood-clot transfers that we see on the shroud are what the Mishnah defines as mingled blood.[12]

Barbet mentions in his book that he believed that while the body was wrapped, it was bathed in a watery atmosphere causing the dry clots on the skin to be damp once more.[13] To verify his suggestion, I added normal saline to each clot. But this only prolonged the transfer of neat clots to cloth from one and a half to two hours. After two hours, when the clots had dried, moistening them did not produce satisfactory transfers (Figure 5). Retrospectively, I can understand why Barbet surmised that the clots were remoistened in the cave. He knew that moist clots are very easily disturbed. He also knew that if a man was taken from the vertical position of crucifixion and placed on a cloth, the clots on his body would be easily disturbed. Finally, he knew that there is no sign of disturbed clots on the shroud.

What Barbet did not realize was that the blood of the shroud is mingled blood. Because there are no signs that the blood marks of the shroud were disturbed, I believe that it is reasonable to make the following assumption: The work of moving the man from the crucified position to the shroud was done by people who took great care not to disturb the moist blood clots that covered the body of this man. Historically, the only people who would make such an effort are the people of Israel. Therefore, this effort suggests that this was a Jewish burial.

In summary, as I did this study, I learned four things about the blood marks of the shroud: (1) I was able to confirm Barbet's observation that blood clots transfer to cloth as mirror images of themselves. (2) The neatness of some of the transfers is likely related to the fact that the man of the shroud died in the vertical position. (3) The ability of clots to transfer to cloth at room temperature is about one and a half to two hours, depending on available moisture. These times coincide closely with the gospel timetable of the death and burial of Jesus. (4) The undisturbed clot transfers seen on the shroud cloth suggest that this was a Jewish burial.

BLOOD ON THE FACE

Chapter Seven

1986

Figure 1

Shroud face,
positive image

For many years the positive image of the shroud face (Figure 1) hung on my office wall. Almost every day I looked across my desk at that face, sometimes partially closing my eyes as I gazed at the image, wondering if the face held some secret. I'll admit that I was looking for something almost magical. During those years, I would always delight in showing any interested observer the blood marks of the face and hair, the contusion under the left eye, and the way the face would seem to follow me as I walked from one side of the room to the other.

In 1986, I discovered something new. It came subtly, gradually, and without magic. Over time, as I would observe the blood of the forehead and hair, I wondered if the blood came out a little too far on either side of the face. I wondered if it were not the same phenomenon as is seen at the off-image blood mark at the left elbow. Eventually I took the life-size picture of the shroud face from the wall and brought it home. I asked my daughters, Catherine and Marguerite, to outline on tracing paper the blood marks of the forehead and hair. I also asked them to trace the position of the eyes and nose. I then had Catherine make a cutout of the tracing, remove the paper within the outlined blood marks, and make holes at the eyes that would be large enough to see through. When she finished, I took her work and went to a mirror and placed the tracing paper with its cutout over my face, aligning the eyes and nose of the figure with my own. As I looked through the eye slits at the reflection of the paper that covered my face, I was stunned by what I saw. Wanting confirmation from an objective observer regarding the reflection in the mirror, I sent the cutout to Alan Adler with the following instructions: "Go to a mirror, then align and wrap the cutout on your face, and let me know what you think you are looking at."

He called back. "When I first saw your cutout, I thought that you had finally lost your mind and had started playing with paper dolls. But I decided that I'd humor you and play along. I went to the mirror to look, and I couldn't believe what I saw. The blood is not on the hair. It's on the sides of the face!" Alan came to the same conclusion as I had. It was as simple as cutting out paper dolls, but the information helps us to better understand the shroud.

Visually reproducing this was fairly simple. All I needed was a bearded man. Reverend Dan Twomey of my own parish volunteered. It was while I was taking the first picture of Father Dan as he was sitting at my dining-room table that I suddenly realized that I had made a mistake. I was not working with a vertical image on the shroud, but with a horizontal image, so I asked him if he would lie down (Figure 2) so that I could retake his picture

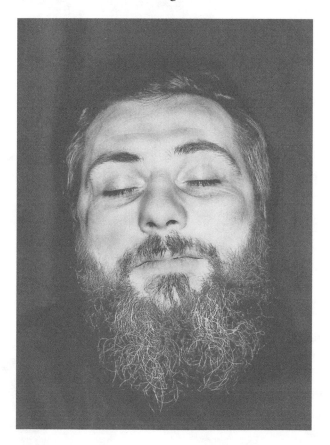

Figure 2

Man's face in a lying position

in the correct position. Using my full-size photograph of the shroud face, we had already prepared another cutout of the blood marks of the face and hair, but this time we used cloth (Figure 3). I draped the cloth with the cutout of the blood marks over Father Dan's face (Figure 4), aligning his eyes and nose with that of the tracing. While the cloth was over his face, I applied paint

Figure 3	Figure 4

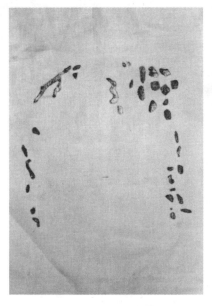 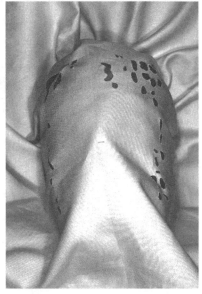

Cutout of the blood marks of the face and hair of the shroud

Cutout of the blood marks draped over a man's face

to his skin through each blood-mark cutout. I then removed the cloth from his face. The painted blood marks graphically demonstrated that all the blood marks seen on the hair of the shroud image had been originally on the face. Yes, they had been on the temples and cheeks of the man who had been under the shroud

(Figure 5). The blood marks are consistent with a cloth having been draped over a man's face covered with moist clots.

These same blood marks of the face also told me something about the facial image: the shroud cloth had been in intimate contact not only with the front of the face but also with the sides of the face (Figure 5). Yet despite the intimate contact that the shroud cloth had with the temples and cheeks, no images of the sides of the face are seen (Figure 1). In contrast, if images had been produced where the shroud cloth came in contact with the sides of the face, the resulting facial image would have been markedly distorted. The cheeks and temples would have extended out to the blood marks seen in the hair. It would have looked like Vignon's experiment, that of the flattened face that Bonnie and I saw in Turin in 1978.

Only now do I finally realize that Vignon's experiment with aloes and ammonia[1] was simply a straightforward contact process. That is why the nose and cheeks of the experiment were broad and distorted. The cloth had touched the sides of the nose and draped over the roundness of the cheeks and temples. That resulted in the accentuated broad flat face. But the nose and cheeks of the shroud are not broadened, and the face of the shroud image is not grotesque. Rather, what you see is the frontal view of a normal face, the same frontal view that you would see of yourself in a mirror or photograph. What does the absence of the images of the sides of the shroud face mean? It means that the shroud image could not possibly have been formed by a cloth-to-body contact process. Then what had caused the image? I did not know, but as time passed, I began to realize that the blood on the face and hair had more to reveal about the image.

As I contemplated the facial image and the graphics of the blood marks, the chasm between the two grew deeper and wider until I could no longer look upon the shroud image in the same way. The key to the puzzle—a puzzle that I previously had not

Figure 5

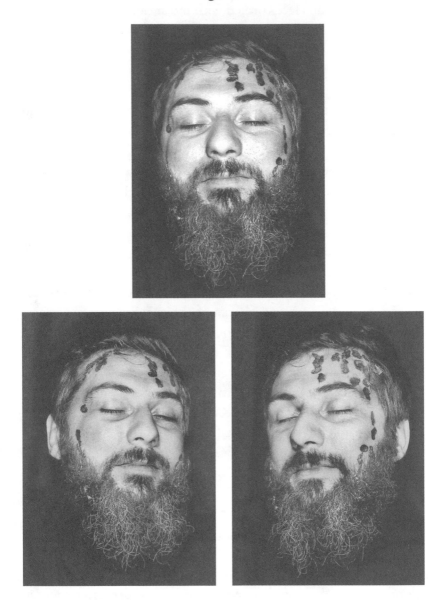

Blood marks painted on the man's face
through the cutout

even known existed—was the spatial relationship of the cloth to the face that it covered. I now understood that to produce the blood marks that are seen on the face and hair of the shroud, the shroud cloth had to be draped over a three-dimensional face that was covered by moist blood clots. Because of this understanding, I began to look at the shroud's facial image from a different point of view. I started to recognize the obvious: the temples and the cheeks of the image do not exhibit the blood marks that had been on the face of the man who had been covered by the shroud. Those blood marks are now out in the hair. Furthermore, if the blood marks were on the face of the shroud image, the final facial image would be more like Figure 5 instead of Figure 1.

The relationship of the blood marks to the facial image (Figure 6) demanded an answer to the following question: What does this lack of congruence say with regard to image formation? It says that image formation did not take place at the time that the cloth was draped over the face. Why? Because the draped cloth that was touching the temples and the cheeks carries the mirror image of the moist blood clots that were originally on the draped man's temples and cheeks. These blood marks are now in the hair that falls along the sides of the face (Figure 1).

Furthermore, and most important, the direct frontal view of the cheeks and temples of the facial image lies in between the blood marks that were originally on the temples of the man draped by the shroud (Figure 6). It seems that the facial image was created not at the time of the draping, but at a time when the cloth was stretched out and a negative photograph of the face appeared on the flattened cloth between the blood marks. The visual information at hand tells its own story. The production of the blood marks and the formation of the body image are much more than two different phenomena each caused by a different process. They really tell us something much more profound: the

Figure 6

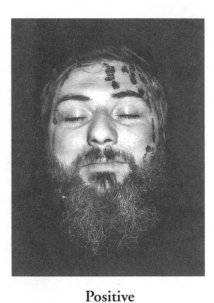

Positive

Negative

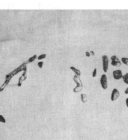

Cutout

Cutout superimposed
over negative

formation of the blood marks and the creation of the image had to have been two separate events, separate in space and separate in time!

Which came first, the blood or the image? Alan Adler discovered that the fibers of cloth that were covered by blood were all white. There were no yellowed image fibers under the blood. Given this, Adler concluded that the blood must have protected the fibers from whatever process caused image formation.[2] Therefore, on a micro level, Adler found that the formation of the blood marks and the creation of the image had a time sequence; they were two separate events, and the blood came first.

In the final analysis, the blood on the face and hair illustrates three important points: (1) The blood demonstrates a pattern that is consistent with that of a cloth having been draped over a supine body. (2) The direction of the blood flows illustrates that the body had previously been in the vertical position. (3) These blood marks are consistent in demonstrating that one process formed the blood marks and that another completely different process created the image. More specifically, most of the blood marks on the cloth are a contact process formed by cloth coming in direct contact with moist blood clots. The image, however, is not a contact mechanism. Finally the blood on the face and the hair uniquely illustrates that the formation of the blood marks and the creation of the image are two separate events, separate in space and separate in time.[3]

CARBON DATING
THE SHROUD

Chapter Eight

———— ❧ ••• ❧ ————

1988

The *New York Times* carried three articles on October 14, 1988. The third paragraph of the first article summed it up:

> *Radiocarbon tests conducted independently by three laboratories this year . . . concluded that the shroud cloth was created between 1260 and 1390.*

Each of the labs tested[1] a piece of the shroud cloth that was not much larger than a postage stamp. These small pieces were obtained from a sample of cloth that had been cut from one end of the fourteen-foot linen. The first *New York Times'* article went on to say that it was theorized that (1) the image was a painting or (2) "that organic residue left on the cloth by some person was discolored by heat and aging to produce a brownish image." In other words, the image was either the work of an artist or a natural phenomenon caused by the cloth coming in contact with the body of a man.

My response to the radiocarbon date is difficult to explain. It is the feeling that one gets when two apparent "truths" collide. Using technical data to make medical decisions has been part of my life. Now, with the carbon-dating information at hand, I made the decision to accept the shroud as a 14th-century artifact. This decision, however, carried with it an unrelenting agitation. The agitation persisted for about six weeks until something happened: I gave another lecture on the shroud.

I began my presentation by stating that carbon dating had proved that the shroud was likely an artistic endeavor of the 14th century. I then went on to show the audience some pictures of the shroud, some of the work of other scientists, and some of my own work. After giving my presentation, I concluded by saying, "Now, who was the artist, and how did he do it?" I then opened the floor to questions.

To my surprise there were no questions regarding an artist or how he did it. All the questions were directed toward carbon dating. I kept insisting that the shroud was a 14th-century cloth, but the audience did not agree. Gradually I began to realize that the people in that audience were reawakening me to reality. At last, in response to their questions, I gave in and said, "Okay, I will have to admit that it is also very difficult for me to believe that an artist did this." As I left that lecture hall, the agitation began to abate.

Gradually I began to reexamine the possibility that the shroud is authentic. The first matter that I dealt with was something that had bothered me for several years, but I had never pursued it: the right forearm of the shroud image was three inches longer than the left, and I had never been satisfied with available explanations. One evening my son, Andre, and I brought Father Donovan's life-size photos of the shroud into my living room and unrolled them onto the floor. Andre and I began our study by taking measurements of the arms. After much discussion and trial and error, we finally found that the difference in the lengths of the forearms of the shroud image was the result of the combination of the bending forward or the extension of the left hand at the wrist and the natural curling of the fingers in the grasp position. Indeed, there was a logical explanation. The difference in the lengths of the forearms was only an optical illusion. (See Appendix A for the details of this study.)

As 1988 faded into 1989, the agitation of two "truths" colliding had abated but still lingered. The *New York Times* had appropriately reported alternative theories in response to the carbon-dating results. I now realized that I had no choice but to directly respond to the carbon-dating results. I had no reason to doubt the work that the laboratories had done.[2, 3] I have a healthy respect for scientific data. However, I have also been trained to question data.

As I turned my attention to the carbon-dating results, I realized that if the shroud is not authentic then it has to be just as the *New York Times* said. It is either an artistic endeavor or a natural phenomenon, the results of the cloth coming into contact with the organic matter of the body of a crucified man. A crucifixion done in the Middle Ages could have been performed the way it had been done to Jesus as described in the Bible. As I looked at both of these theoretical alternatives, I felt that I understood the shroud as well as any theorist. I decided to look at the data as I would look at any information used in making a medical decision about one of my patients.

I started with the first theoretical possibility presented in the *New York Times:* the shroud image is an artistic endeavor. I reviewed what I had learned about the image. In 1933, Barbet made the observation that there was no paint on the image area. He confirmed his observation with Enrie's photographs taken at seven times magnification. Miller's micrographs taken in 1978 also show areas of the image. These micrographs, at 64x magnification, demonstrate no debris. This is not what I would expect if the image were painted. There is no doubt that Miller's micrographs visually reconfirm Barbet's initial observations made in 1933. Paint is not found on the shroud image.

Also, Eric Jumper and his colleagues, as firsthand witnesses, teased at the shroud image fibers and noted that only the top-most fibers of a thread carry the yellow fibers that make up the image. When teasing down below the yellowed top fibers of a thread, Jumper noted that the fibers below the first layer of fibers were white. The image penetrates down into the thread only one fiber deep. During his observation, Jumper also noted that each fiber that caused the image was the same intensity of color. In other words, each white fiber was darkened to a specific yellow hue. He found that the only reason why certain areas were darker than others was that there were more of the yellowed fibers in one area than in another. As Jumper said, "It's like the dots of newspaper print. If you want to make an area darker, you put in more dots." In computer language, these dots would be the pixels on a monochrome screen or the dots per inch of a laser printer. In other words, the shroud image on the micro level is compa-rable to modern technological methods of producing 20th-century images. It is not 14th-century technology.

Finally, Alan Adler studied the chemistry of these fibers. They are made of cellulose. He discovered that the chemical reaction that caused the cellulose to be yellowed was a degrada-tive process, as one sees in the aging of linen. Adler understood how the fiber can be yellowed, but he did not know how the image was formed and neither does anyone else. Alan Adler best summed up his thoughts on his findings when he said, "For a painter to have created this image, he would have needed a paint-brush the size of a fiber which is less than half the width of a human hair." I wrestled with all of this information over and over again. I thought about Barbet's studies and my own. I thought about the negative image. I even wondered how a 14th-century artist could have checked the progress of his negative technique without the benefit of a 19th-century invention called photog-raphy. Enough! For me there is no longer any doubt: the shroud image is not an artistic endeavor.

I then turned to the second theory that was reported by the *New York Times:* the image was formed when "organic residue left on the cloth by some person was discolored by heat and aging to produce a brownish image." They were saying that image formation was caused by a contact process. It is a two-step process: (1) The cloth came in contact with organic matter on the body of a man. (2) Heat and the aging of the residue left on the cloth resulted in the formation of the image. This sounds like a plausible naturally occurring method of image formation.

In fact, Barbet's work plus the studies that I had done with the blood marks had convinced me that the blood marks are a natural phenomenon caused by the cloth coming in contact with the moist blood clots of a crucified man. However, the image is a different event. The studies of the blood on the face and the blood off the left elbow have made this evident. If the image had been made by a contact process, it would be distorted, just as distorted as the Vignon image that I had seen in the small Turin museum in 1978. Rather, the image is a separate event from that of the blood marks, separate in place and separate in time. The facial image is in between the blood marks of the face, as if the cloth, after having been draped over the face, had been straightened out and a negative image of the face developed on the flattened cloth, as if it were a photographic plate. This is true of the entire image, testified by the blood off the left elbow. Therefore, this negative image of the shroud, this snapshot of a man, is not a simple contact process. Rather, the image-forming process is more comparable to the modern technology of photography.

I now knew where I stood with regard to the second theory reported by the *New York Times*. The image formed by cloth coming into contact with the organic matter on the body of a man is simply not a viable theory. Furthermore, millions of people for thousands of years have been buried in cloth, yet only the Shroud of Turin carries such an image.[4]

So if the image is not a painting and its formation is unexplainable and the accompanying blood marks are a natural phenomenon, where did that leave me? It left me with an image of a man crucified as Jesus was. It left me with an unexplained image, an unexplained 14th-century event if one is to accept carbon dating.

Again, I stood back to look at the information that was at hand and realized that the shroud could only be the end result of one of three possibilities. The shroud was either one of the two alternative theories as outlined in the *New York Times* or it was the shroud of Jesus of Nazareth. There were no other alternatives. Carbon dating forced the issue in the direction of either artistic endeavor or natural phenomenon. Yet the data that others as well as myself had accumulated over the years were in conflict with either an artistic endeavor or a natural phenomenon as explanations of the formation of the image. Therefore, the unexplained image with its accompanying blood marks pointed toward the third alternative, toward an event that occurred in the first century.

Was I to ignore the information pointing toward the first century? Did carbon dating invalidate the other facts that were now at hand? I now had to ask myself if carbon dating was the only 20th-century science done on the shroud. After giving this some thought, it seemed to me that the dating of the shroud was the most sought after information. Without a doubt, the carbon dating was the best-known scientific testing that had been done on the shroud. However, it was not the only science that had been applied to the shroud. It was no more scientific than Frei's work done with pollen grains. It was no more scientific than Adler's chemistry, Miller's micrographs, Jumper's teasing at the fibers, or Barbet's medical observations. Science is a body of knowledge that is systematically gathered, and that knowledge is used to find answers to questions. In the end, answers have to satisfy the available information.

When I began stacking up the evidence, I found a long list of facts that elucidate an unexplained image and blood marks that point to a first-century event. That which pointed to a 14th-century artwork or to a 14th-century natural phenomenon is limited to carbon dating. My decision was becoming easier and easier. Finally I decided that the carbon-dating story is comparable to being at the bedside of a patient in respiratory distress. The patient's respirations are rapid and shallow, the muscles of the chest are fatigued, the pulse is fast, and the blood pressure is dropping; the prognosis is grave. A decision has to be made regarding the respiratory support of this patient who is very ill with pneumonia. The blood-gas report, which details the oxygen and carbon dioxide content of the patient's blood, has returned. The results are normal. Looking only at the blood-gas data one would believe that the patient is stable and that no intervention is warranted. However, the blood gases do not fit the clinical picture that is seen at the bedside; the clinical situation demands that the blood gases be repeated. But now there is no more time for further testing: the clinical situation requires that the patient be immediately placed on a respirator.

Like the patient in respiratory distress, the shroud, the blood marks, and the image tell their own story. Like the blood gases, the carbon-dating results on the shroud do not fit the rest of the data. Science demands that the entire carbon-dating issue be revisited, and in this case, there is time for further testing.

Now the agitation was gone. Again I could look upon the shroud with its blood marks and image in the way that I have come to understand it. The blood marks are the imprints of moist blood clots that came into contact with the cloth as it was used to shroud the supine body of a crucified man. The subtle detail of the clot at the left elbow is consistent with a previously active blood flow of crucifixion as the Mishnah describes it. The presence of intact blood clots suggests that this was a Jewish burial. But most important was *the creation of the negative image of a man* (Figure 1) found among these blood marks. It was a separate event, not made by contact, and *not made by human hands* (Figure 2).

The Creation of the Negative Image of a Man . . .

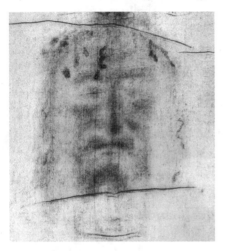

Figure 1:

The actual shroud
is a negative image

. . . Not Made by Human Hands

Figure 2:

The negative plate
of the shroud
is a positive image

In 1988–89, with the information that I then had in hand, I was convinced that carbon dating should be repeated—and this conviction persuaded me to continue on with my studies. Since that time, even more data has become available regarding the origin of the shroud as well as the radiocarbon dating test of 1988.

Whangers' and Danin's recent work (1997) concludes that there are, on the non-image areas of the shroud, very faint images of spring flora from the Jerusalem area. Frei (1978) had previously discovered on the shroud, pollen grains, some of which come from some of the same type of flora seen on the cloth. The above provides proof that the shroud had a pre-European, pre-14th century history. Furthermore, Whangers' and Danin's study presents evidence that the shroud originated in the Jerusalem area at the spring of the year—the time of Passover—the time of Easter (see pages 47–48).

Since 1988–89, new information on radiocarbon dating of the shroud is also available.[5] An excellent 1989 article, "Carbon Dating the Shroud of Turin," explains that the radiocarbon scientists prepared a protocol requiring six samples of the shroud and the use of seven laboratories in order to assure the best result. The reality is that the protocol was abandoned and the scientists, through no fault of their own,[6] were given only one sample of the shroud.[7] This sample was portioned and three pieces were then given to three radiocarbon dating labs, each lab receiving one piece of this one sample.

Regarding taking samples from a study object, the carbon dating article further states: "Archaeologists should be sure the samples they take are representative and homogeneous with respect to the questions being asked."[8] In the case of the shroud, the question being asked is the date of origin of the shroud. The heart of this test which uses samples is to be certain that the samples reflect the whole. In this case the one sample taken from the shroud should be "representative" of and "homogeneous" with the rest of the cloth. If it isn't, no matter how good the dating test is, there will be a sampling bias which would jeopardize the accuracy of the test. Now, in asking if the one sample taken from the shroud was or was not representative of the rest of the cloth, one has to remember that no other samples were taken from other parts of the cloth. Therefore, there is no basis for comparison to assure that the first and only sample taken is or is not "homogeneous" or "representative" of the rest of the cloth.

Dr. Alan Adler (1996) has done an examination of a piece of the shroud sample used for radiocarbon dating, comparing it to the non-image area of the cloth by Fourier Transform Infrared microspectrophotometry and by a scanning electron microprobe. The results clearly indicate differences in chemical composition: "The radiocarbon samples are not representative of the non-image samples that comprise the bulk of the cloth."[9] Therefore, the sample given to the radiocarbon scientists does not follow their own criteria—that a sample be "representative" and "homogeneous."

In conclusion, the accuracy* of the radiocarbon test results is questionable. Using the appropriate protocol, the radiocarbon test needs to be repeated.

---

* The precision of the radiocarbon dating results done by the three labs is not in question, but it is the accuracy[10] that is in question. For those interested in further discussion, see the three references cited.[11]

THE SHADOWS
OF THE
IMAGE

Chapter Nine

———— ❧ ··•·· ☙ ————

1989

I had thought about it since 1986 when I did my paper on the blood marks on the face. However, I had never put my thoughts down in writing until now. It was just three weeks before the 1989 Paris International Shroud Symposium when I was preparing my presentation. As I held up to the light a transparency of the shroud face (Figure 1), I was reminded that the image and the blood marks were telling their own story. It was all so logical, and it seemed as if it had all been planned for the human mind to contemplate. All the directions were contained in the face of the image. Not the magic that I had once imagined, but logical, reproducible, simple answers to profound questions.

In 1986, when the insight first came, I was in my living room comparing the negative photograph of Father Dan's face to my transparency of the shroud face as it is seen on the cloth. As I held the negative of Father Dan's face (Figure 2) up to the light, I was struck by the fact that his image was not similar to the shroud image.

On the shroud face, there was light around the eyes, under the nose, at the lips; Father Dan's face was a bland gray, with no striking differences of shades of gray as seen on the shroud image. Also, the hair of Father Dan came out light, as opposed to the

Figure 1   Figure 2

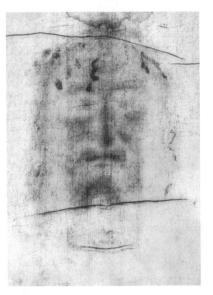
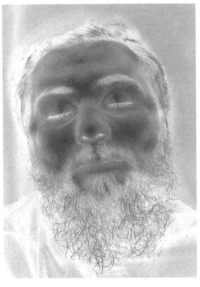

Shroud face,   Negative image of face,
negative image   lying position

dark hair of the shroud image. What was wrong? Knowing that the shroud image was thought to have been a negative since Pia's first photograph in 1898, I made every effort to reproduce a negative that would simulate it. I even placed the bearded volunteer in the supine position so as to best imitate the image of the shroud. Disappointed in my findings, I began to look through all my negatives until I came across another negative of Father Dan's face. In awe, I sat there. Then I stood up, and out of reverence for what I saw, I slowly backed away. There was no denying it. The light areas around the eyes, between the lips, and under the nose, were all there. Father Dan's face (Figure 3) had all the same characteristics as that of the shroud face except for the shading of the hair. This negative of Father Dan was photographed differently (lighting and position) from the original. Part of that

Figure 1   Figure 3

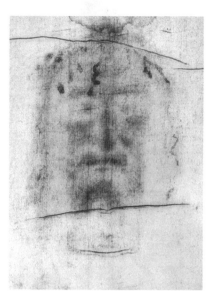   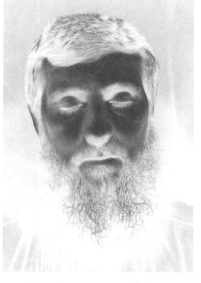

Shroud face,   Negative image of face,
negative image   upright position

difference was the beginning of an understanding of the shroud image that I could never have predicted in 10 lifetimes.

In taking pictures of Father Dan, it was my original intention to photograph him lying on his back, the position that I felt best simulated the image of the man of the shroud. However, by mistake, I first took a picture of Father Dan's face in the upright position. It was this negative of Father Dan's face in the upright position that corresponded to the face of the shroud image. The shadows of the shroud's facial image are, therefore, not those of a man lying on his back. Rather, the shadows of the face of the shroud image are those of a man in an upright position.

I later made a study of the negatives of Father Dan's face. After trial and error, the conclusions were simple enough, and they were easily reproducible. If a source of light is from above,

Figure 4

Figure 5

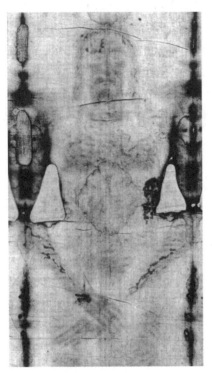 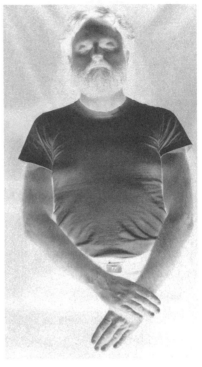

Frontal image
of the shroud,
negative image

Negative image of a man,
upright position,
light coming from above

as it usually is in daily life, and a person is upright, there are shadows (light areas) around the eyes, under the nose, and about the lips (Figure 3). (The shroud face carries other shadows that correspond to facial swellings caused by a beating. See Barbet Chapter 1.) If an individual is supine and the light source is from above, there are virtually no shadows (Figure 2). After further observation, I found other shadows (light areas) on the shroud image (Figure 4). There are shadows under the hair, at the neck, under the pectoral muscles of the chest, and under the hands. All

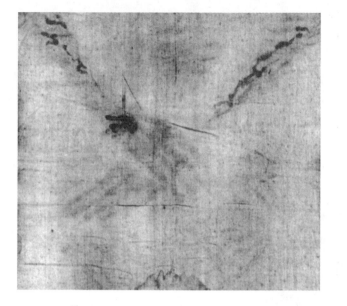

Figure 6

**Hands
of the
shroud
image,
negative
image**

these shadows (light areas) seen on the shroud image can be reproduced. As long as the light is from above and the man is upright, the shadows (light areas) on the negative image of a man (Figure 5) are similar to those of the shroud. Shadows (light areas) of the negative can be seen under the neck, under the pectorals, and at the hands (Figure 5). If we look at the hands of the shroud image (Figure 6), we can easily see the shadows (light areas) between the fingers and on the underside of the hand with the visible wrist wound. This is nicely reproduced on an upright negative image of a man with the light source coming from above (Figure 7). In contrast, there are no shadows (light areas) seen on the negative image of the hands when the man is in the supine (lying) position and the light is from above (Figure 8). Therefore, all these shadows of the image of the shroud are consistent with a negative photograph of a man in the upright position with the source of light coming from above. (I am simply reporting what is visible on the shroud image and not proposing a theory of image formation.)

Figure 7

**Negative image
of hands,
upright position**

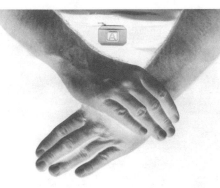

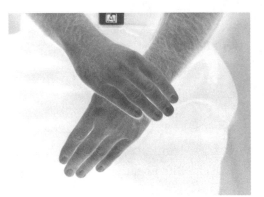

Figure 8

**Negative image
of hands,
lying position**

As I was organizing these thoughts for my Paris presentation, I looked to see if there were consistencies other than the shadows that would correspond to an upright man. As I looked over the frontal image of the shroud, I suddenly became aware of the obvious. Again, another answer was found at the face of the image. This time it was the hair. The hair flows down on both sides of the face following the force of gravity. Looking at the back image I could see that the same was true. The hair flows over the shoulders and down the back.

In order to confirm these findings, I did a simple experiment. Figures 9, 10, 11A, 11B, and 12 tell the story. Figures 9 and 10 are the negative images of the front and back of an upright volunteer with long hair. The hair falls along the sides of the face

Figure 9

Negative front image
of long hair,
upright position

Figure 10

Negative back image
of long hair,
upright position

Figure 11A

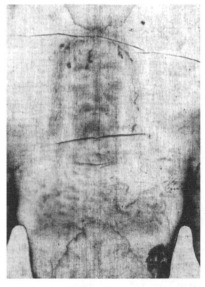

Hair of the front image,
negative image

Figure 11B

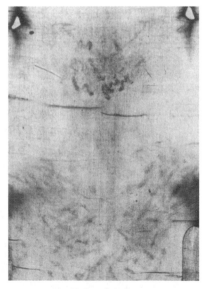

Hair of the back image,
negative image

Figure 9   Figure 12

Negative front image   Negative front image
of long hair,   of long hair,
upright position   lying position

to the shoulders and down the back. The hair of these images is consistent with that of the shroud (Figures 11A and 11B). Figure 12 is the negative image of the same person (taken at another time) in the supine, or lying, position. The hair falls to the ground rather than to the shoulders. It is simple enough. Long hair responds to gravitational force and takes on a typical appearance that is familiar to everyone. The hair of the man of the shroud is that of an upright man.

I remember photographing the volunteer of Figures 9 and 10 outside. The day was cloudy. The diffuse light was coming from above. With this in mind, it is interesting to note that these negatives have similar shadow areas around the eyes, under the nose, between the lips, and under the hair, as is seen on the shroud image (Figures 11A and B).

Again, I looked at the back image and on doing so, I remembered my visit to a small museum in 1978, when Dorothy Crispino pointed out ". . . the roundness of the muscles as if the

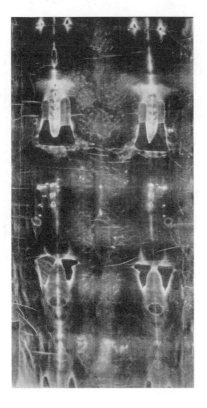

Figure 13

Back image
of the shroud,
positive image
backlighted

Figure 14

Soles of the feet
of the shroud,
positive image
backlighted

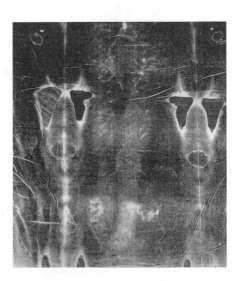

Figure 15A	Figure 1	Figure 15B
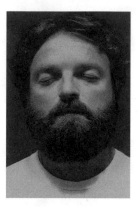		
Man with dark brown hair, positive image	**Shroud face, negative image**	**Man with dark brown hair, negative image**

person were right in front of you" (Figure 13). The muscles of the back may not all be perfectly round,[1] but there is no doubt that the back image is ". . . as if the person were right in front of you." For me there is no longer any question: this image is that of an upright man.

Upright, yes, but not standing. The soles of the feet (Figure 14) indicate that the image of the man of the shroud is not in the standing position. This image of the feet reminded me of another experience that occurred shortly after my return from Turin in 1978. I had just finished giving a lecture to a group of physicians on Barbet's studies of the shroud. After the lecture, one of the physicians approached me. He looked puzzled and said emphatically, "It seems as if the man is suspended in midair." At the time, I said "Yes." But I really did not understand what he had seen. It took me years to see what he had seen that evening: the image of a man who is upright and unsupported.

One more thing had to be understood before I left for Paris. In the negative, Father Dan's hair is light and that of the shroud

Figure 16A   Figure 1   Figure 16B

      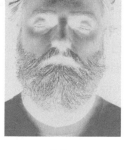

| Man with white hair, positive image | Shroud face, negative image | Man with white hair, negative image |

is dark. Father Dan has dark brown hair, with two streaks of white in his beard. These streaks of white beard are dark in the negative, as dark as is the hair of the man of the shroud image. Does that mean that the man of the shroud has white hair?

Father Dan had left the area, and I needed to find another bearded man. Reverend John Arens gave a hesitating "Yes" when I asked him. I purchased white hair coloring for his dark brown hair and took pictures of him before and after. I got the negatives back just before leaving for Paris. Father John's dark brown hair (Figure 15A) was light on the negative (Figure 15B). His white hair (Figure 16A), as expected, came out dark (Figure 16B).[2] The pictures themselves explain that if the shroud image is a negative, as has been the premise since 1898, then I could not make any exceptions to that premise. If we take this one step further and make the assumption that the shroud image is a negative picture of the man who had been originally under this cloth, then the logical conclusion has to be made: the man of the shroud had either white or light blond hair.

After our arrival in Paris, I had the opportunity to think through the work that I had been compelled to pursue. As I sat in an open cafe, I gathered my thoughts in preparation for my presentation. Gradually, over the years, the shroud image and its blood marks had revealed their own story. Because the blood marks on the hair and the face were not congruent with the facial image, I had realized that the cause of the blood marks and the cause of the image were two separate events, separate in space and separate in time. Furthermore, the shadows of the face and the flow of the hair convinced me that the image of the man of the shroud was upright. However, the upright position of the image was not in harmony with the accompanying blood marks, which were consistent with a crucified man having been placed in the supine position between the folds of this long cloth. As a result, I could no longer look upon the shroud image as the picture of a scourged, crucified man lying on his back, shrouded, and ready for burial. The bridge had been crossed, and there was no turning back. Yes, I was looking at a bloodstained cloth that had covered the body of a man who had been scourged and crucified. But now among the blood marks was the remarkable image of a suspended man whose white hair falls to his shoulders and whose feet do not touch the ground (Figure 17). With these thoughts in mind, I sipped the last of my coffee and knew that I was ready to give my paper.[3]

But after my presentation, I found myself asking, "What does all this mean?"

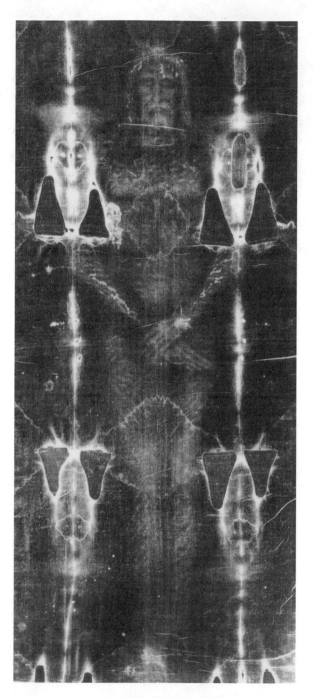

Figure 17: Front of shroud, positive image

JOSEPHUS:
THE IMAGE
OF A MAN

Chapter Ten

$\text{---}\,\infty\!\!\!\!\text{)}\cdots\text{(}\infty\,\text{---}$

1990

Early on in my study of the shroud, I turned to the Bible for answers to questions that I had concerning the cloth. At first, I found no answers. However, as I continued to read the Bible, I slowly began to realize a truth that ran through each line of this incredible work. Every word (except Luke) had been written by the people of Israel. It was the story of the Jewish people, a people who believed in one invisible God. It was the story of the Jews, lived by Jews, and told by Jews from Genesis through Revelation. To be able to understand it, I had to start thinking like a Jew, a first-century Jew.

I quickly learned that a Jew of the first century was a Jew of the Pentateuch, so I read the first five books of the Bible, also known as the Torah, or the Law. I read Genesis through Numbers, some of the Prophets, and the four gospels. After carefully reading the death and resurrection stories of each of the four gospels, I asked myself why John's* account of the events

---

* Tradition places John, son of Zebedee, as the author of the gospel of John. In modern times, the authorship of John has been questioned by some biblical scholars:

a. Raymond Brown, *The Community of the Beloved Disciple.* (New York: Paulist Press, 1979), 33–34.

b. George R. Beasley-Murray, *Word Biblical Commentary,* vol. 36 (John) (Waco, Texas: Word Books, 1987), lxxiv–lxxv.

However in spite of the differences of opinion proposed by scholars regarding authorship, there is little disagreement that, *"one principal disciple . . .* gave shape to the stories and discourses now found in the Fourth Gospel." (See: Raymond Brown, *The Gospel According to John,* vol. 29 (I–XII) (New York: Doubleday and Co., Inc., 1970), CI.)[1]

was so different from the others. The most practical reason seemed to be the obvious one. He was the only one of the four gospel writers who was there. He was an eyewitness. John wrote about what he saw. Because of this, I decided to make an attempt to think as John might have thought. I started by asking myself what I knew about John. He lived as a Jew, thought as a Jew, and was influenced by the words of the Pentateuch and the Prophets. He was immersed in the history of his time and region, and he was one of Jesus' closest friends.

For me, the immediate question was, If John had seen the shroud, with its bloodstained image, why did he not just say so? Incredibly, there was an answer to that question in Josephus' history of the Jews. Josephus lived from A.D. 37 to 100. His understanding of the Jewish world paralleled John's life as John wrote his gospel. The following excerpt from Josephus' writings told me something very important about the times in which John lived:

> 1. *Now Caius Caesar did so grossly abuse the fortune he had arrived at, as to take himself to be a god, and to desire to be so called also, and to cut off those of the greatest nobility out of his country. He also extended his impiety as far as the Jews. Accordingly, he sent Petronius with an army to Jerusalem, to place his statues in the temple, and commanded him that, in case the Jews would not admit of them, he should slay those that opposed it, and carry all the rest of the nation into captivity: but God concerned himself with these his commands.*

Josephus goes on to relate the Jews' response:

> 3. *But now the Jews got together in great numbers with their wives and children into that plain*

that was by Ptolemais, and made supplication to Petronius, first for their laws, and, in the next place, for themselves. So he was prevailed upon by the multitude of the supplicants, and by their supplications, and left his army and the statues at Ptolemais, and then went forward into Galilee, and called together the multitude and all the men of note to Tiberias, and showed them the power of the Romans, and the threatenings of Caesar; and, besides this, proved that their petition was unreasonable, because while all the nations in subjection to them had placed the images of Caesar in their several cities, among the rest of their gods, for them alone to oppose it, was almost like the behaviour of revolters, and was injurious to Caesar.

Josephus further relates the Jews' strict adherence to their laws:

4. *And when they insisted on their law, and the custom of their country, and how it was not only not permitted them to make either an image of God, or indeed of a man, and to put it in any despicable part of their country, much less in the temple itself, Petronius replied, "And am not I also," said he, "bound to keep the law of my own lord? For if I transgress it, and spare you, it is but just that I perish; while he that sent me, and not I, will commence a war against you; for I am under command as well as you." Hereupon the whole multitude cried out that they were ready to suffer for their law. Petronius then quieted them, and said to them, "Will you then make war against Caesar?" The Jews said, "We offer sacrifices twice every day for Caesar, and for*

*the Roman people;" but that if he would place
the images among them, he must first sacrifice
the whole Jewish nation; and that they were
ready to expose themselves, together with their
children and wives, to be slain. At this Petronius
was astonished, and pitied them, on account of
the inexpressible sense of religion the men were
under, and that courage of theirs which made
them ready to die for it; so they were dismissed
without success.*[2]

Josephus' story was clear: It was "not permitted them to
make either an image of God, or indeed of a man." For the Jews,
the image of God was forbidden, so forbidden that the Jews were
prepared to die rather than have the image of God in their
country. Moreover, Josephus was making it clear that not only
was the image of God forbidden, but also the image of man: "or
indeed of a man." Why did the Jews forbid images in their
country? The most obvious biblical source to that question is
found in Exodus. It is the second of the Ten Commandments.

*You shall not make yourself a carved image or any
likeness of anything in heaven or on earth beneath
or in the waters under the earth; you shall not bow
down to them or serve them. For I, Yahweh your
God, am a jealous God and I punish the father's
fault in the sons, the grandsons, and the great-
grandsons of those who hate me; but I show kindness
to thousands of those who love me and keep my
commandments.*

Exodus 20: 4–6

John was a Jew and a person of his time, and he knew the
Torah, which was the Law. He knew that images of man were
considered objects of idolatry. He also knew the sensitivities of

his countrymen, the Jewish people, and he would have known that the image that we see on the shroud, the image "of a man," would have been sought out and destroyed if its existence had been known. That images are forbidden was driven home to me when I read from the Mishnah (the oral tradition of Moses) the following passage regarding images: "All images are forbidden because they are worshipped once a year."[3]

If John did have possession of the shroud, I could now understand why he would not mention it in his gospel. Such an admission would have resulted in the shroud's destruction.

THE FOURTH GOSPEL

Chapter Eleven

————— ❧ ·•· ❧ —————

1990–1992

Now that I understood why John could not mention the shroud in his gospel, I asked another question: If John had the shroud, or knew of its whereabouts, did he make a subtle attempt to communicate that fact to later generations who might look to his gospel in search of the shroud's origin? In asking such a question, I was taking an intellectual leap in assuming that John would actually hide something. Was it legitimate to make such an assumption? To my surprise, I found that this assumption was reasonable. Why? The first clue came as I read the three letters of John, the gospel writer. The last two sentences found at the end of two of his letters (2 John and 3 John) were almost identical in text and meaning. John wrote, "I have much to write to you, but I would rather not write with pen and ink; instead I hope to see you soon, and we will talk together face to face" (3 John:13–14). For me this was evidence that John held back knowledge of events that could not be told to all. He evidently needed to keep secrets and would go to great lengths to keep certain events within a privileged circle of believers: ". . . instead I hope to see you soon, and we will talk together face to face."[1]

When I discussed this issue with Reverend Dan Twomey, he explained that the Bible is full of secrets. One reason that biblical authors wrote with double meanings was that it enabled them to inform their inner circle of believers, while at the same time escape persecution from the ruling authorities. Our conversation reminded me of a quotation from Daniel: "I heard but could not understand; so I said, 'My lord, what shall be the outcome of these things?' He said, 'Go your way, Daniel, for the words are to remain secret and sealed until the time of the end'" (Daniel 12:8–9). Indeed, the Bible does hold secrets.

I now knew that techniques of writing biblical secrets had been in existence long before the Gospel of John's time. He, as well as any one else who read the Scriptures, had the opportunity to acquire the skill of passing on written secrets. Considering that John kept secrets, it is certainly conceivable that he could have included messages in his written gospel that would be understood only by an inner circle of trusted believers.

What seemed at first to be vague coincidences in John's gospel slowly fell into a pattern, a pattern so well designed that I could no longer ignore the message. The thought that initiated my pursuit came unexpectedly. My subconscious had been working for me; a quotation from John's gospel came to mind: ". . . and he saw and believed" (John 20:8). As I contemplated these words, I asked myself "Saw what?" For the moment, the answer seemed obvious to me. It had to have been the shroud, but I was not sure why. The impulse to pursue the subject was strong enough to cause me to turn all my efforts toward the study of John's gospel.

In chapter 20, the resurrection narrative, John brings the reader to the climax of his gospel by first explaining that Mary Magdalene had found an empty tomb concluding that the body had been taken. She reported her findings to the other disciples. Peter and John immediately raced to the tomb. John reached the tomb first, looked in, and saw the linen cloths.[2] Then Simon Peter reached the tomb and entered ahead of John. As Peter entered the tomb, he also saw the linen cloths and the cloth that was over Jesus' head rolled in a place by itself. John then followed Peter into the tomb, ". . . and he saw and believed." These words—". . . and he saw and believed" (John 20:8)—were for John and for his gospel the climax of his story. In this short sentence, we are told of John's personal moment of understanding that caused him to believe. For me, it was the beginning of an insight that I felt compelled to follow.

I remembered something that I had read many years before about "and he saw and believed": the verbs *saw* and *believed* have no objects. What did John see, and what did he believe? From my recollection, I remember that I was amazed to find that the object of John's belief was not the resurrection. Why? Because after his exclamation of belief, John's very next statement is ". . . for as yet they did not understand the scripture, that he must rise from the dead" (John 20:9). In other words, John makes a special effort to tell us that he believed, but what he believed was not that Jesus had resurrected. As I read the rest of chapter 20, the object of the verb *believed* became evident. John's exclamation of belief on that early morning was not his belief in Jesus' resurrection. In fact, what he believed was much more profound than resurrection. What he believed on that early morning was that Jesus was the Son of God. Why do we know that? We know because John tells us exactly what his belief is.

John tells us over and over again that Jesus is the Son of God. From the moment of John's statement of belief in the tomb to the end of chapter 20, his story revolves about the personal encounters of Mary Magdalene, the disciples, and Thomas with the risen Jesus. John tells of these encounters with the risen Jesus, ". . . so that you may come to believe that Jesus is . . . the Son of God" (John 20:31). This theme is specifically underlined in Jesus' encounter with Thomas, who refused to believe the other disciples when they told him that Jesus had appeared to them. Jesus later presented himself to Thomas and said to him, "Do not doubt but believe" (John 20:27). Thomas's reply to Jesus was "My

Lord and my God!" (John 20:28). Thomas's exclamation reveals that his belief went way beyond that of resurrection. That Jesus is the Son of God is in fact the predominant theme of John's entire gospel. We know this for certain in that John makes a point of introducing this theme at the beginning of his gospel in chapter 1: "And the Word became flesh and lived among us, and we have seen his glory, the glory as of a father's only son, full of grace and truth" (John 1:14).

The question is: If it took an encounter with the risen Jesus for Mary Magdalene, Thomas, and the disciples to believe that Jesus was the Son of God, why did John believe with no encounter with the resurrected Jesus?[3] Why did he believe at the very moment that he entered the empty tomb? Since Mary Magdalene had already emotionally prepared John by saying "They have taken the Lord out of the tomb" (John 20:2), what impact could an empty tomb have had on him? What could he have seen in that tomb that caused him to conclude that Jesus is the Son of God? What was the object of his statement "he saw"? What did he see? An empty tomb, yes. The linen cloths, yes. But was this enough to make him believe that Jesus is the Son of God, especially if he did not understand at that moment, as he stood in the tomb, that Jesus was to rise from the dead?

John tells us the object of his verb *believe,* but does he tell us the object of his verb *saw?* Interestingly enough, just before making his statement of belief, he describes the linen cloths in the tomb:

> He [John] bent down to look in and saw the linen wrappings lying there, but he did not go in. Then Simon Peter came, following him, and went into the tomb. He [Peter] saw the linen wrappings lying there, and the cloth that had been on Jesus' head, not lying with the linen wrappings but rolled up in a place by itself.
>
> *John 20:5–7*

John describes the linens twice and makes the point that they have been seen by two witnesses. By Jewish law (Deuteronomy 17:6 and Matthew 18:16), this would confirm the existence of the linens. The linen cloths are seen first through his eyes and then through Peter's eyes. There is no doubt that John has focused on the linen cloths, including the one rolled in a place by itself. Why is this important? Because following this emphasis regarding the linen cloths comes the climactic sentence of his gospel, John's moment of understanding: "Then the other disciple [John], who reached the tomb first, also went in, and he saw and believed" (John 20:8).

After entering the tomb, John "saw" something that moved him to believe that Jesus is the Son of God. John had to have seen something awesome in that tomb to have come to such a conclusion. Considering his emphasis on the linen cloths prior to his moment of understanding, it would seem reasonable to postulate that the linen had something to do with what John "saw." In chapter 20, John tells us why Mary Magdalene, the disciples, and Thomas believed—because they saw the resurrected Jesus. However, throughout chapter 20, John never tells us what he saw in the tomb to cause him to believe. What did he see? (See Appendix B for further discussion of this question.) Was it the image of Jesus on the linen shroud? Would this cause him to believe?

In order for me to answer these questions, I had to understand how John would react to the image of the shroud. I had to understand his point of view. To do that, I had to think like a first-century Jew. To the first-century Jew, and to the believing Orthodox Jew of today, it was and is forbidden for a Jew to possess the image of a man (like the shroud image). John is a Jew of the Pentateuch, and he was well aware of God's second commandment that forbids images. From Josephus (A.D. 37–100) I knew that first-century Jews took the second commandment seriously and that they would rather be "slain" than have "an image of God, or indeed of a man" in their presence.[4]

To further understand the reason that the Jews have this understanding of images, especially those of man, I returned to Genesis, the first book of the Pentateuch. There I found the words "So God created humankind in his image, in the image of God he created them; male and female he created them" (Genesis 1:27). John would have been familiar with these words, and he would have also known the corollary in the same way that Josephus knew it and in the same way that all believing Jews have known it—that the image of man represents the image of God.

With the above in mind, could it be, when John entered the tomb, that he saw not only the linen cloths but also saw on the cloth that covered Jesus' body, the image of a man? Could it be that he recognized the image as the image of his Master, of his friend Jesus? Knowing that a first-century Jew believes that the image of a man represents the image of God, I asked the following questions: Could it be that the discovery of the image caused him to exclaim, "He saw and believed"? Could it be that the discovery of the image on the burial cloth moved John to believe that Jesus is the Son of God?

As exciting as this theory was to me, there was one major stumbling block. From John's perspective as a first-century Jew, images of man were considered objects of idolatry and were forbidden.

> *You shall not make yourself a carved image or any*
> *likeness of anything in heaven or on earth beneath*
> *or in the waters under the earth.*
> *Exodus 20:4*

However, as I wrestled with this thought, I recalled an experiment that I had done several years before—placing simulated blood through the cut-outs of the cloth that I had placed on Father Dan's face. At the moment that I removed the cloth from his blood-marked face, I remembered imagining that John would have seen lots of dried blood along with these same moist blood clots on the temples and cheeks of Jesus' face before he was draped by the burial cloth. Later, in the tomb, John would have seen these same blood marks on the shroud. But this time he would have seen the image of Jesus' face in between the blood marks that previously had been on his temples and cheeks. Therefore, John would have had all the information necessary to understand that the blood marks on the shroud cloth were one event and that the accompanying image was another.

John's closeness to the crucifixion, the burial, and the subsequent finding of the image on the shroud at the tomb would have brought him to realize that this image was something special. John would have seen the sequence of these events as they occurred in time, while we have been attempting to understand them by going back in time. Having been denied the priviledge of witnessing the same sequence of events as John would have seen them, it has taken centuries for us to understand what we are seeing on the cloth. However, from John's perspective it would have taken him but an instant to know that this image was not made by human hands. John, the Jew, would have also known that what is made by hands is from man (Deuteronomy 4:28), and what is not made by hands is from God (Hebrews 9:11).[5] Therefore, he would have known the biblical significance of his discovery: he would understand that this image was made by God and was not forbidden.

Encouraged that John may have indeed seen the shroud, I decided to look for other clues that might refer to the shroud in John's gospel. Looking back at chapter 19, I reviewed the description of Jesus' burial. Jesus was buried "according to the burial custom of the Jews" (John 19:40). I now knew what the first-century Jews meant by the words "burial custom of the Jews." In that Jesus died a violent death, the mingled blood (life-blood) remained on the body, and the body was not washed but was wrapped in a linen sheet and buried. In telling his readers how Jesus was buried, was John preparing his readers for what to expect to see on the linen cloth: the blood marks of a violent death? All through chapter 19, John describes in detail the tortures that Jesus underwent, all of which are found on the shroud: "flogged," "wove a crown of thorns and put it on his head," "striking him on the face," "they crucified him," "they did not break his legs. Instead, one of the soldiers pierced his side with a spear, and at once blood and water came out" (John 19:1, 2, 3, 18, 33–34). Was John describing the image and blood marks of the shroud for future generations?

As I read chapter 20, I found another message alluding to the shroud that seemed to have been carefully woven between the lines of John's gospel. To me it was as if John had masterfully combined two scenes to send his readers a single undebatable message as to what happened to the shroud. In scene one, after Mary Magdalene tells the disciples that the body of Jesus has been taken, John and Peter race to the empty tomb, and on looking into the tomb, John sees the linen cloths. At the end of the scene, John tells of their departure from the tomb, "Then the disciples returned to their homes" (John 20:10).

Immediately following this statement, John starts scene two and reintroduces Mary Magdalene who stands weeping outside the tomb:

> As she wept, she bent over to look into the tomb; and she saw two angels in white, sitting where the body of Jesus had been lying, one at the head and the other at the feet.
>
> *John 20:11–12*

Mary's investigation of the tomb parallels that of John's from the previous scene: "He [John] bent down to look in" (John 20:5); "she bent over to look into the tomb" (John 20:11). John saw the linen cloths; Mary Magdalene saw two angels. At face value, John describes what is seen in both scenes. However, taking this a step further, is John saying that Mary Magdalene does not see the linen cloths, the linen cloths that were so important to John on entering the tomb that he had two witnesses describe them? Finally, is John telling the reader that she does not see the linen cloths when "she bent over to look" because they were taken by John and Peter when "the disciples returned to their homes" (John 20:10)?

In summary John believes that Jesus is the Son of God. He has written his gospel so that his readers will understand why he believes this, so that they may believe as well. The cornerstone of that belief was the resurrection. John readily supplies witnesses, Mary Magdalene, the disciples, and Thomas, who all saw the risen Jesus and, therefore, had come to believe. However, John does something else which is not so easily understood. He tells us that he came to his belief before having seen the risen Jesus. He tells us that it was something that he saw in the tomb that caused him to believe, but he never directly reveals what it was. John has created a mystery.[6] Was this not his intent?

This mystery has caused me to ask what it was he saw that brought him to believe that Jesus is the Son of God. As a result, the scriptural study of John's gospel, approached from the perspective of a first-century Jew, has produced evidence that suggests that John saw the shroud image. What makes this argument compelling is knowing that there is a shroud image not made by human hands. If John did indeed see this image of Jesus in the tomb, then there is no longer any mystery as to why he exclaimed, "he saw and believed."

THE VISION
OF DANIEL

Chapter Twelve

—◦◦ ·•· ◦◦—

1993–Present

Long before I began searching for biblical answers pertaining to a man suspended in midair, I must admit that I had already come to my own understanding regarding the significance of the upright negative image. It was in 1986, when I was comparing Father Dan's upright negative to the shroud image, that I first realized that the image was not that of a man lying in burial. Rather, this was the reflection of an upright man.

Over the years my understanding of the image has slowly matured, but the awe has never abated. Yes, this image carries a beaten face, closed eyes, scourge marks, a chest wound, and the wounds of crucifixion—the image of death. But now I also knew that the creation of the image was a separate event from the blood marks that were caused by contact, a separate event not made by human hands. I also knew that the shadows of the image indicate that the body is upright. For me, this evidence, evidence I never believed would exist, has caused me to contemplate, to wonder, and to hopefully understand the truth about this image. This image of a man whose white hair falls to his shoulders, and whose feet do not touch the ground—is this the reflection of the transition from death to life? Is this the moment of the resurrection?

When I was preparing for my 1989 Paris presentation, I looked for biblical evidence that might refer to a suspended upright man with light colored hair. As it turned out, my first and only biblical reference describing Jesus as a white-haired man came quite by accident. The event occurred just days before leaving for Paris. Father John and I were trying to determine if the hair of the image of the shroud was light in color. Father John was combing the white coloring into his hair in preparation for our pictures when he said, "There is a quotation in Revelation, chapter 1, that states that Jesus had white hair." I quickly went to the Bible and turned to Revelation. I read what John had seen in a vision: "I saw one like the Son of Man. . . . His head and his hair were white as white wool, white as snow" (Revelation 1:13–14).

Before I finished the reading, I found myself asking who the "Son of Man" was. I learned that Jesus referred to himself as the Son of Man. With this information and with further study of chapter 1 of Revelation, I was able to define whom John was describing in his vision: he was speaking of the risen Jesus. Was it more than just a coincidence that both the image of the man of the shroud and the risen Jesus of John's vision had light hair?[1]

With regard to the upright man, my biblical search was quite different and was eventually very revealing. However, as I started looking through the Gospel of John, I felt that there was a major obstacle: with only the negative image at his disposal, John would not have realized that the shroud figure was upright. Then how could he have related this information to his inner circle of believers? He could not and he did not. I came to find that this communication was left to someone else.

Sometime close to my departure for Paris in 1989, while I was preparing for my presentation, I turned to chapter 12 of John's gospel and found the following words of Jesus: "And I, when I am lifted up from the earth, will draw all people to myself" (John 12:32). It was the word *lifted* that brought forth an image that seemed to define what I saw on the shroud. By the shadows that are seen on the face and the hands of the shroud image and by the flow of his hair, the man of the shroud is upright. By the position of his feet, he is upright, but not standing. Is this not the definition of a suspended man? Is not a suspended man also the definition of a lifted man? The more I thought of it, the more reasonable it seemed. Was the suspended man of the shroud the reflection of the lifted Jesus of John 12:32? As I contemplated this question, I remembered my disappointment when I first realized that the upright man was not standing. At that time the standing position would have been so much more realistic to me. But now, as I looked at verse 32 in John, I could hardly believe how relevant the shroud image was to the words of Jesus. Was Jesus predicting his resurrection?

As exciting as it was to come across this verse in the Gospel of John, there was another quotation that tempered my enthusiasm. It was verse 33, the very next verse in John's gospel: "He said this to indicate the kind of death he was to die," implying that in verse 32, Jesus was talking of his crucifixion and not of his resurrection. Fortunately, my curiosity caused me to persist. Somehow, it just did not make sense that Jesus would be talking about his crucifixion alone. That represented death, an end with no future vision in sight. How could the imagery of a dead man on a cross draw all people to himself? Could he have meant more than simply predicting his death by crucifixion?

I looked to an author well known for his expert commentaries on the Gospel of John. On reading Raymond E. Brown's introduction to his commentary, I came across the following sentence: "The culmination of his career is when he is lifted up toward heaven in death and resurrection to draw all men to himself (xii 32)."[2] Once I read those words, I knew that I wasn't alone in speculating that lifted meant more than being lifted on the cross. Brown argues that Jesus' claim of drawing all people to himself once he is lifted cannot be verified in crucifixion alone. Brown believes that "being lifted up" includes Jesus' being lifted in crucifixion, resurrection, and ascension. Brown also believes that this moment of time was predicted in Isaiah: "Behold my servant shall prosper: he shall be lifted up and glorified exceedingly" (Isaiah 52:13). Brown's rationale is compelling, and those seeking further information should refer to his text.[3] Like Barbet, whose insights on the shroud brought me to want to know more, Brown's insights on the lifted Jesus encouraged me to pursue this matter further.

Brown's work also brought my attention to three quotations in the Gospel of John where Jesus uses the expression "lifted up." I took all three passages to Paris. I also brought along a fourth, the one from Revelation on white hair. I included all four of them in my Paris presentation in 1989:

> *"No one has ascended into heaven except the one who descended from heaven, the Son of Man. And just as Moses lifted up the serpent in the wilderness, so must the Son of Man be lifted up, that whoever believes in him may have eternal life."*
> *John 3:13–15*

> *"When you have lifted up the Son of Man, then you will realize that I am he, and that I do nothing on my own, but I speak these things as the Father instructed me."*
> *John 8:28*

> *"And I, when I am lifted up from the earth, will draw all people to myself."*
> *John 12:32*

Then I turned to see whose voice it was that spoke
to me, and on turning I saw seven golden lamp-
stands, and in the midst of the lampstands I saw one
like the Son of Man, clothed with a long robe and
with a golden sash across his chest. His head and his
hair were white as white wool, white as snow.
Revelation 1:12–14

While in Paris, I noticed that in three out of the four quotations, the words *Son of Man* were mentioned. Other than knowing that Jesus referred to himself as the Son of Man, I did not understand the meaning of these words. For the moment, the coincidence piqued my interest, but the matter was pushed aside in light of a more pressing situation—the preparation of my presentation.

In 1993, as I started to rewrite this chapter, I decided to read John's gospel again. I eventually came across chapters 3, 8, and 12 and the words of Jesus on being lifted up. I again noted that the quotations in chapters 3 and 8 included "Son of Man"; chapter 12:32 did not. But when I read chapter 12 in its entirety, I came across the following passage: "We have heard from the law that the Messiah remains forever. How can you say that the Son of Man must be lifted up? Who is this Son of Man?" (John 12:34). Upon reading those words, I asked myself, what is this—the Son of Man? Is Jesus talking about the Son of Man being lifted up again for a third time? I read chapter 12 again and found the following words of Jesus in the introduction of this same scene: "The hour has come for the Son of Man to be glorified" (John 12:23). Indeed, for the third time, Jesus was talking about the Son of Man. I finally came to the realization that Jesus was persisting in making the connection between the Son of Man and being lifted up. Why was he doing this? I knew that Jesus called himself the Son of Man, but

I could not grasp the significance of the title Son of Man. However, I did sense that it might be central to what he was saying. Before going on, I had to try to understand the meaning of Son of Man.

Commentaries from the 1966 Jerusalem Bible directed me to the prophet Daniel (Matthew 8:20—commentary on verse 20 is 8h). It was there that I found the origin of the concept of the Son of Man:

> *"As I watched in the night visions, I saw one like a son of man coming with the clouds of heaven. And he came to the Ancient One and was presented before him. To him was given dominion and glory and kingship, that all peoples, nations, and languages should serve him. His dominion is an everlasting dominion that shall not pass away, and his kingship is one that shall never be destroyed."*[4]
> *Daniel 7:13–14*

Using the same source, the *Jerusalem Bible* (Daniel 7:13—commentary on verse 13 is 7k—and Matthew 8:20—commentary on verse 20 is 8h), I found that the Son of Man is the Messiah. The coming of the Messiah is a major theme of the Prophets and his arrival is the most important anticipated event of the Jewish nation.

Now the question was: Do the Jewish sources also consider the son of man from Daniel (Daniel 7:13–14) to be the Messiah? Looking for an answer, Bonnie and I returned to the Hebrew library where I had started doing my research many years before. In perusing the works on Daniel, I came across Rashi, a well-known and respected rabbinic authority of the eleventh century, who believed that the "son of man" of Daniel's vision (Daniel 7:13) was the King Messiah.[5] This information, later supported by many other rabbinic sources,[6] confirmed that the son of man of Daniel's vision is the Messiah.

The next question was: Did the Jews at the time of Jesus believe that the Son of Man was the Messiah? When I looked back at John's chapter 12, I could see that there was no doubt that the Son of Man was considered the Messiah by the Jews. Why? In response to Jesus' words, "And I, when I am lifted up from the earth, will draw all people to myself" (John 12:32), the crowd responded, "We have heard from the law that the Messiah remains forever. How can you say that the Son of Man must be lifted up? Who is this Son of Man?" (John 12:34). From their response, the Jews understood that the words *Son of Man* referred to the Messiah. Their objection was that once the Messiah came to earth, why should he be lifted up above the earth since the Law states that the Messiah is to remain forever.[7]

I now understood the significance of the title Son of Man. Obviously, by referring to himself as the Son of Man, Jesus was stating that he was the Messiah. But what connection did this have with being lifted up? Why was Jesus so persistent in using this title every time he talked about being lifted up? I read chapter 12 of John's gospel and chapter 7 of Daniel again and again. Slowly I began to see that many of the words of chapter 12 in John were similar to those of chapter 7 in Daniel:

> *"The hour has come for the **Son of Man** to be glorified."*
>
> *John 12:23*

> *"To **him** [the son of man] was given dominion and glory and kingship."*
>
> *Daniel 7:14*

> *". . . those who hate their life in this world will keep it for **eternal life**."*
>
> *John 12:25*

> *"His dominion is an **everlasting dominion**."*
>
> *Daniel 7:14*

*". . . where I am, there will my **servant** be also . . .*
*And I . . . will draw **all people** to myself."*
                                    John 12:26 and 32

*". . . that **all peoples**, nations, and languages should*
serve him."
                                              Daniel 7:14

It seemed as if there was a parallel between the scriptures of
John and Daniel. Was Jesus (John 12:22–32) referring to Daniel's
vision (Daniel 7:13–14)? Months after I first asked that question,
I was reading John's chapter 12 when the word *judgment* of verse
31 caused me to quickly turn the pages of my Bible to chapter 7
of Daniel. In verse 10, there was the same word: *judgment.*

Until now, I had concentrated on verses 13 and 14 of
Daniel's chapter 7; the earlier verses of the chapter had eluded
me. Indeed, it was the full story of Daniel's vision that eventually
provided the necessary information for understanding Jesus'
words in John's chapter 12. In his vision, Daniel saw the four
winds of heaven stirring up the sea, and from the sea came four
beasts. These beasts were terrifying. They dominated everyone
about them. Then Daniel saw the Ancient One taking his throne
before a great multitude who attended him. The court sat in
judgment, and the most terrifying beast was put to death;
the rest had their dominion taken away. As Daniel continued
to watch, he saw one like a "son of man" come with the clouds
of heaven; this man was presented to the Ancient One. To him
was given the service of all peoples and a dominion that would
never end.

With Daniel's vision in mind, I returned to John's chapter
12. I stopped when I read the following words of Jesus:

> *"Now is the judgment of this world; now the ruler*
> *of this world will be driven out. And I, when I am*

lifted up from the earth, will draw all people to myself."

John 12:31–32

To me this sounded very similar to Daniel. I decided to compare Daniel to John, verse to verse:

The court sat in judgment, and the books were opened.

Daniel 7:10

"Now is the judgment of this world."

John 12:31

"And as I watched, the beast was put to death, and its body destroyed and given over to be burned with fire. As for the rest of the beasts, their dominion was taken away."

Daniel 7:11–12

". . . now the ruler of this world will be driven out."

John 12:31

"I saw one like a son of man coming with the clouds of heaven."

Daniel 7:13

"And I, when I am lifted up from the earth . . ."

John 12:32

"To him was given dominion and glory and kingship, that all peoples, nations, and languages should serve him."

Daniel 7:14

". . . will draw all people to myself."

John 12:32

Concept for concept and in perfect sequence, Jesus is summarizing the vision of Daniel. Moreover, the crowd's response confirms that it knows to whom Jesus is alluding:

The crowd answered him, "We have heard from the law that the Messiah remains forever. How can you say that the Son of Man must be lifted up? Who is this Son of Man?"

John 12:34

The crowd recognizes that Jesus is referring to the "son of man" of Daniel's vision but as previously stated, the crowd does not understand why he is to be lifted up once he has come to earth.

As I came to realize that Jesus (John 12) was summarizing the vision of Daniel (Daniel 7), I stopped to reflect upon what brought me to these texts. It was the suspended image of the shroud. Was there a meaningful connection between the texts and the image? Traditionally, the words *lifted up* have been interpreted as the foretelling of the crucifixion (John 12:32–33). But now, as Brown had indicated, there was more to being lifted up than simply crucifixion. Therefore, I returned to chapters 3, 8, and 12 of John, keeping in mind the relationship between being lifted up and the coming of the "son of man" in the vision of Daniel.

As I read these chapters, I did not find any consistent story line, message, or relationship. Looking back now, I believe that I did not want to get involved with attempting to further understand the Scriptures. I felt that it was too complicated, and anyway, I had no business doing this. I was not a scripture scholar. However, for some reason, I felt compelled to read chapters 3, 8, and 12 again. It was at that reading that the story line finally became obvious. That experience taught me that, like the shroud, the Scriptures belong to all of us, and with a little effort, we can understand them.

In chapter 3, Jesus is in Jerusalem where Nicodemus, a Pharisee, meets him. Jesus tells Nicodemus that "no one can see the kingdom of God without being born from above" (John 3:3). He explains that for one to enter the kingdom of God one must be born of the Spirit: "What is born of the flesh is flesh, and what is born of the Spirit is spirit. . . . You must be born from above" (John 3:6–7). Jesus is explaining that there are two worlds: that of the flesh, which we know ends with the last heartbeat, and that of the spirit, which we know is eternal. The spirit of eternal life can come only from the world above—heaven. With the imagery of two worlds in place, Jesus then introduces the Son of Man, emphasizing his ability to access these two worlds: "No one has ascended into heaven except the one who descended from heaven, the Son of Man" (John 3:13). This is followed immediately by his first mention of being lifted: "And just as Moses lifted up the serpent in the wilderness, so must the Son of Man be lifted up, that whoever believes in him may have eternal life" (John 3:14–15). It was while reading John's third chapter that I started to realize that each time Jesus speaks of being lifted, he gives a specific message. His first message is "that whoever believes in him [the Son of Man] may have eternal life" (John 3:15). In other words, belief in the Son of Man confers to the men and women of this world the Spirit of eternal life.

In chapter 8, we find Jesus teaching in the treasury of the Temple. In talking to the crowd, he again develops the imagery of two worlds: "You are from below, I am from above; you are of this world, I am not of this world" (John 8:23). Just as in chapter 3, once the imagery of two worlds is in place, Jesus then introduces the Son of Man: "When you have lifted up the Son of Man, then you will realize that I am he, and that I do nothing on my own, but I speak these things as the Father instructed me" (John 8:28).

In this second introduction of the lifted Son of Man, Jesus relates a second message: once the Son of Man is lifted, then all will know that Jesus is "he," the Son of Man, and that he is doing the will of the Father. The crowd evidently understood his message, for John writes: "As he was saying these things, many believed in him" (John 8:30). However, this understanding did not come from the knowledge of an event that had not yet occurred, the crucifixion, but came from knowledge that the crowd shared in common—Daniel's vision of the "son of man."

In chapter 12, Jesus is in Jerusalem during the festival time. He announces to the crowd that the "hour" when the Son of Man is to be "glorified" has come (John 12:23). This time, the two worlds are at hand. Jesus says:

> "And what should I say—'Father, save me from this hour'? No, it is for this reason that I have come to this hour. Father, glorify your name." Then a voice came from heaven, "I have glorified it, and I will glorify it again." The crowd standing there heard it and said that it was thunder. Others said, "An angel has spoken to him." Jesus answered, "This voice has come for your sake, not for mine."
>
> John 12:27–30

Again the same pattern is followed, and after the introduction of the two worlds, Jesus brings forth for the third time the concept of the lifted Son of Man. His listeners are all well versed in their Jewish faith, and they are all familiar with the "son of man" of Daniel's vision. To this crowd, Jesus states his third message. Jesus announces (John 12:31–32) that the event predicted in Daniel's vision (Daniel 7:10–14) is to be fulfilled "now" (John 12:31). This is the "hour . . . for the Son of Man to be glorified" (John 12:23).

Once I focused on the word *glory,* I better understood the event predicted in Daniel and John. In Daniel and John, the word *glory* points to the fulfillment of an event that comes to its completion as the Son of Man reaches his destination. To completely understand this event, I had to ask the question, What is that destination? In Daniel, it is spelled out:

> *"I saw one like a son of man coming with the clouds of heaven. And he came to the Ancient One and was presented before him. To him was given dominion and glory and kingship, that all peoples, nations, and languages should serve him."*
>
> Daniel 7:13–14

In John, it is only implied that Jesus is lifted up to the Ancient One—to the Father:

> *"And I, when I am lifted up from the earth, will draw all people to myself."*
>
> John 12:32

However, the meaning of Jesus' words are confirmed in his encounter with Mary Magdalene on that early morning at the tomb:

> *Jesus said to her, "Do not hold on to me, because I have not yet ascended to the Father. But go to my brothers and say to them, 'I am ascending to my Father and your Father, to my God and your God.'"*
>
> John 20:17

Once Jesus is lifted up from this world to the world above where he meets the Father and is glorified, the event is completed.

I was now convinced that the lifting of Jesus in chapter 12 did indeed go far beyond the prediction of crucifixion. In fact, as Brown observed, the words of Jesus throughout the Gospel of John emphasize the upward movement of Jesus, the Son of Man, back to the Father:

> *"Then what if you were to see the Son of Man ascending to where he was before?"*
>
> *John 6:62*

After reading the Gospel of Matthew, I came to understand the Son of Man from another perspective. In describing the last days, Jesus said:[8]

> *"Then the sign of the Son of Man will appear in heaven, and then all the tribes of the earth will mourn, and they will see 'the Son of Man coming on the clouds of heaven.'"*
>
> *Matthew 24:30*

Reflecting on this verse from Matthew's gospel caused me to realize that Jesus is talking to his listeners about the "sign" of the Son of Man, a sign that his audience is already familiar with. Accompanying the concept of the Son of Man is always the imagery of a man coming on the clouds of heaven. This vision is the "sign" of the Son of Man.

In contemplating the information that was now at hand, I realized that the meaning of the suspended man of the shroud was becoming evident. Most relevant to understanding this imagery were the following verses from John and Daniel:

> *"And I, when I am lifted up from the earth . . ."*
>
> *John 12:32*

"I saw one like a son of man coming with the clouds of heaven."

Daniel 7:13

In both situations, the Son of Man is coming into his glory (John 12:23 and Daniel 7:14). In both situations, the Son of Man is above the earth (John 12:32 and Daniel 7:13). Indeed, Daniel and John project the same imagery: that of a man above the earth. On the shroud, we see the image of a man whose hair falls to his shoulders and his feet do not touch the ground. On the shroud, we see the very same imagery that we read about in Daniel and in John, that of a man above the earth. Yes, I was coming to understand the reality of what I was looking at on the shroud, and what was making the shroud understandable were the words of the Bible. What was becoming evident is that the image of the suspended man is more than a reflection of the resurrection. Rather, this image belongs to the "hour" of "glory," for it is a reflection of the culmination of the long-awaited biblical event that was first predicted in Daniel and then in John. That event was the coming of the Son of Man—Jesus—to the Ancient One—the Father, resulting in the Son of Man's glory and kingship over an everlasting dominion that shall never be destroyed. This image of the suspended man is the sign of the Son of Man. It is the sign of the Messiah.

"What sign are you going to give us then, so that we may see it and believe you?"

John 6:30

"Then what if you were to see the Son of Man ascending to where he was before?"

John 6:62

"See, I am doing a new deed, even now it comes to light; can you not see it?"

Isaiah 43:19

Epilogue

—⌇⟡ ·✦· ⟡⌇—

Many years ago when I first began studying the shroud, a rabbi asked me, "Why do you study this cloth?" I said, "Rabbi, I study this cloth because it brings me to study the Word of God." He responded with emphasis, "If it brings you to study the Word of God, then you should study this cloth." His words have been with me ever since.

Over these years, I have gradually come to realize that the understanding that we have of the last days of Jesus in Jerusalem has come to us through the Chosen People. What fascinates me is that if these events had occurred in another place, at another time, and in another culture, these very same events would not have been understood. They would have taken place in the world unrecognized and would have simply passed away. It was only because the Jewish people understood these events in the context of the Pentateuch and the Prophets, that we understand the meaning of the life of Jesus.

The same can be said for the pursuit of the study of the shroud. It is only after one looks at the shroud through the mind of a first-century Jew that its full meaning becomes apparent. Studying the blood of the shroud without understanding the laws concerning blood that God gave to his people leaves us with only blood stains. However, understanding the blood from the perspective of a Jew brings our understanding of this same blood to its highest meaning: it is life-blood, the blood of atonement (Leviticus 17:11).

The study of the image of the shroud is intriguing, simply because we cannot scientifically explain its origin. However, through the eyes of a Jew, the image of this man takes on a profound meaning. With regard to the origin of the image, that which is not made by the hands of man is made by God (Deuteronomy 4:28 and Hebrews 9:11). With regard to the image itself, the image of man is the image of God, for God made man in his own image (Genesis 1:27).

The image of the upright, suspended man found among the blood stains on the shroud is fascinating. Why? Because this finding is intellectually exciting to anyone who contemplates the possibility that this image reflects the moment of the resurrection. But even this pales when one finally understands the meaning of the suspended man through the eyes of the Jewish people. This sign—that of the man above the earth, that of "one like a son of man coming with the clouds of heaven" (Daniel 7:13)—is the fulfillment of the predicted biblical event of the coming of the Messiah who has created for us "an everlasting dominion that shall not pass away" (Daniel 7:14).

Having lived for these past 20 years on the fine line between Christianity and Judaism, I have come to better understand the truth that lies within these faiths. The truth is that all we know about Christianity comes from the disciples of Jesus, practically all Jews. As we stand here today seeking to understand as best we can the Shroud of Turin, so it was in the past. In Jerusalem, at the time of Jesus, men and women witnessed the events as they happened. These people sought to understand what they saw in the light of their Jewish faith. With this information at hand, one

is compelled to ask the question "Is Christianity a Jewish event?"
Possibly the answer to this question comes from Jesus:

"Salvation comes from the Jews."

John 4:22

*"Master, now you are dismissing your servant in
peace, according to your word; for my eyes have seen
your salvation, which you have prepared in the
presence of all peoples, a light for revelation to the
Gentiles and for glory to your people Israel."*

Luke 2:29–32

APPENDICES

Appendix A

The Difference in the Length of the Arms Is an Optical Illusion[1]

My son Andre and I began our study by taking measurements of the arms. We used the photographic negative of the shroud image showing the positive image of the man (Figure 1). The

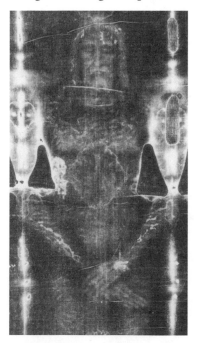

Figure 1

Front image of the shroud, positive image

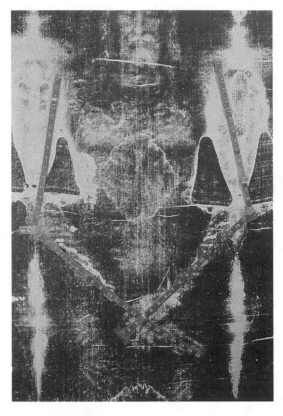

Figure 2

Upper arms
of the
shroud image
are both
approximately
16 inches.
The right forearm
is 21 inches;
the left is
18 inches,
positive image.

image of the upper arms had been burned away in the fire of 1532, so we had to calculate an approximate length, considering both the size of the subject as well as what we could determine from the remaining anatomy. We calculated that the upper arms were both sixteen inches long and that the right forearm was twenty-one inches while the left forearm measured eighteen inches. Thus, the discrepancy of three inches between the right and left forearms was confirmed (Figure 2).

Andre and I compared the measurements of the arms of the shroud to my own measurements. We took the measurements of my arms in the same way that we tried to estimate them on the full-scale image of the shroud. My upper arms were fifteen inches as measured from the top of my shoulder to the tip of my elbow. My forearms were 20 inches when measured from the tip of my elbow to the end of my middle finger. My upper arms are only one inch shorter than those of the shroud image. The same is true of my forearms when comparing them to the longer forearm of the shroud image. These measurements of the shroud image easily fall within the normal range. We then determined the measurements of another volunteer who was smaller in stature. Using a smaller volunteer did not matter in that we were more interested in looking for the reason for the difference in the length of the forearms of the shroud image as opposed to looking at the exact differences in measurement. The upper arms were 14 inches, and the forearms were 18 inches (Figure 3). At that point we had a data base but we did not have an answer.

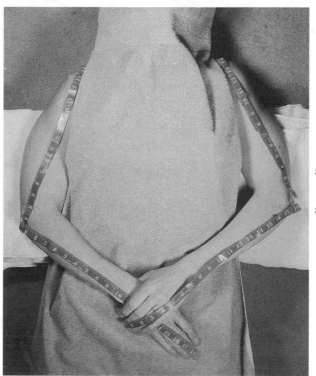

Figure 3

Upper arms are 14 inches; the forearms are 18 inches.

Figure 4

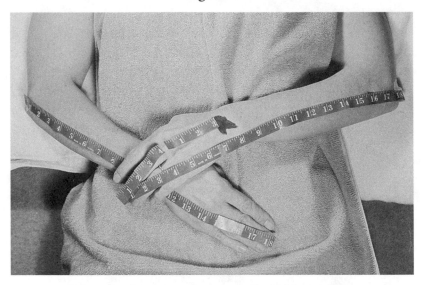

Distance between the center knuckle and the
wrist wound is three inches.
The length of the middle finger is four inches.
The overall length of the left forearm is 18 inches.

Andre and I looked for possible solutions. All at once it
seemed so simple. Could it be that the left forearm was shorter
because the left elbow image had been burned off in the fire? All
I had to do was to extend the left forearm outward by three
inches and determine the theoretical position of the elbow in the
burn area. In extending the elbow into the burn area I found that
the upper arm had to be displaced upward. However, there was
no corresponding anatomical indication that the shoulder had
been lifted or shrugged, so this solution was wrong.

Since an upward shift of the shoulder could not be the cause,
only the areas of the hand and wrist could account for the three-
inch difference. As I looked at the hand and wrist, something
caused me to ask, "What if the hand is bent forward or extended

at the wrist, and the fingers are bent around the other wrist?" I clenched my right wrist with my left hand. I then extended or bent forward my left hand at the wrist. There it was. The altered position of my hand looked very much like the shroud image. Now all I needed were the measurements.

We added a wound mark on the left wrist of the volunteer and then made measurements with the wrist and the fingers being held out straight (Figure 4). We measured the middle finger of the left hand from its tip to the knuckle. It was four inches. We then measured from the knuckle of the middle finger to the wound. It measured three inches. We repeated the same measurements with the left hand bent forward or extended at the wrist and with the fingers of the left hand grasping the right wrist (Figure 5). We again measured the distance between the knuckle of the middle finger to the wound as a straight line, not following the contour of the hand. It was now two inches instead of three inches. Doing the same for the middle finger, we found that the middle finger was now three inches instead of four inches. Furthermore, we found that by bending the hand forward at the wrist and curling the fingers, the combined effect caused an overall shortening of the left forearm and hand by about three inches, giving it a length of 15 inches instead of 18 inches.

We then compared Figure 5 to the shroud image of Figure 6 and saw the similarities of the measurements of the left hand and arm. Once we understood, it was simple, and we could now easily see that the different lengths of the forearms of the shroud image were the result of the combination of the bending forward or the extension of the left hand at the wrist and the natural curling of the fingers in the grasp position. At this point, Andre and I concluded that the difference in the lengths of the forearms of the shroud image was only an optical illusion. The forearms were the same length.

Figure 5

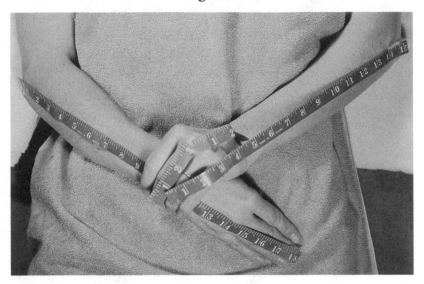

**Left wrist is extended and the fingers are
curled around the right wrist:
knuckle-to-wound distance is two inches and
middle finger length is three inches.
The overall forearm length is 15 inches.**

The measurements fit, but something else left a marked impression. It was the subtlety of the anatomical position of the left hand and the wrist. In comparing Figure 5 with Figure 6, I could see that the upper part (thumb side) and lower portion (little finger side) of the hand are bent upward. Figure 4 does not show the upward slant of the hand because the hand is not extended at the wrist. It is the extension, or the forward bending, of the left hand at the wrist that causes this subtle, but precise, anatomical position of the hand to occur.

Figure 6

Left hand knuckle-to-wound distance is two inches
and the finger length is three inches.
The overall length is 18 inches,
positive image.

Appendix B

————— ⸙ ··•· ⸙ —————

What Did John See?

A possible answer as to what John saw in the tomb began to evolve as I read John's gospel again. In chapter 19, the death narrative, John tells us that the Jews wanted the bodies down from the crosses before the Sabbath, which was the beginning of the Passover. They had asked Pilate to have the legs of the crucified broken in order to hasten their deaths and thus have them removed from the crosses before the Passover began. Pilate granted their wish, and the legs of the two men who had been crucified with Jesus were broken, but on coming to Jesus, the Roman soldiers found that he was already dead so they did not break his legs. Instead, one of them pierced his side and from it came blood and water. Immediately following his description of the dead Jesus, John tells us, "He who saw this has testified so that you also may believe" (John 19:35). It was this quote that caused me to stop, reminding me of "he saw and believed" (chapter 20:8). The similarity was obvious. John elected to use the three words *he, saw,* and *believed* in both chapters. Why? His use of similar words caused me to suspect that John might be attempting to have his readers connect these scenes in a special way.

John refers to himself at least four times in the Gospel of John, each time referring to himself as "he": 13:25, 19:35, 20:8, and 21:20. On two of these occasions "he" is a witness to the most important events of his entire story. The first "he" is used in chapter 19 at the death of Jesus. John tells the reader that "he" has related this description of the dead Jesus so that the reader "also may believe." In chapter 20, the word "he" is used for the second time. It occurs at the discovery of something in the tomb that caused John to "believe."

Is John's use of *he* in both of these scenes his way of tying the two stories together? The words "He who saw this has testified so that you also may believe" (John 19:35) may be the key to that supposition. According to John, what he saw in chapter 19—his description of the dead Jesus—should also cause his reader to "believe" that Jesus is the Son of God. Yet we know that John had not even come to his own moment of belief until three days later when he was in the tomb and "he saw and believed" (John 20:8). Why should his reader believe at a moment in time that precedes John's own belief?

As I contemplated this question, I asked myself, "Could John be expecting his reader of the future to understand what he is talking about once the reader has been made aware of the shroud, its blood marks, and its image?" Is John trying to tell his reader that his description of the dead Jesus in chapter 19, causing his reader to "also believe," is the same thing that caused John to believe in chapter 20? In other words, is John saying that his description of the dead Jesus in chapter 19 is the object of his verb *saw* on entering the tomb in chapter 20?

In order for me to answer these questions, I had to fully understand what John was describing in chapter 19. I had to understand it through John's eyes, the eyes and mind of a first-century Jew. I asked myself, "What is it that John saw in chapter 19 that would cause a first-century Jew to 'believe' that Jesus is the Son of God?" What did John see? John saw the following: "But when they came to Jesus and saw that he was already dead, they did not break his legs. Instead, one of the soldiers pierced his side with a spear, and at once blood and water came out" (John 19:33–34). What is it about this description of the events that occurred at the death of Jesus, the climax of John's crucifixion story, that could cause a first-century Jew to believe that Jesus is the Son of God?

John is describing a visual experience that was familiar to his contemporaries who lived at a time when crucifixion was common. When John said, "But when they came to Jesus and saw that he was already dead, they did not break his legs" (John 19:33), the readers of his day would visualize the intact body of the crucified Jesus, instead of the contorted body of a man with broken, twisted legs as was the case of the other two who were crucified with him. John concluded his description with "Instead, one of the soldiers pierced his side with a spear, and at once blood and water came out" (John 19:34). Here again, as a firsthand witness, John was describing what he saw for his contemporaries and for his future believers: a crucified man who had been pierced and from whose body flowed both blood and water.[1] Does John's description sound familiar? Is he describing what is seen on the shroud, the unbroken crucified body of a man who has been pierced? John concludes the death scene of Jesus with the following quotations from Scripture: "None of his bones shall be broken" (John 19:36) and "They will look on the one whom they have pierced" (John 19:37). He explains that "these things occurred so that scripture might be fulfilled" (John 19:36).

Yet with this scene, described as the fulfillment of the Scriptures (Exodus 12:46, Zechariah 12:10),[2] John did not come to his moment of belief. That moment only came three days later when he entered the tomb (John 20:8). Then why should this scene cause his readers to believe? Furthermore, why did John choose this moment, these words, this description, that so vividly bring to mind the image of the pierced man of the shroud, to be the time for his readers to believe as well? The real question is, "Does John use these words of Scripture to describe to his future readers what they will see when they look upon the shroud?" Is he saying "they will look on" the unbroken, crucified body of a man who has been "pierced"? Is John saying to his inner circle of trusted believers and to those readers of the future who will eventually have the shroud in hand, that what "he saw" in chapter 20 that caused him to "believe" is what he has described in chapter 19 "so that you may also believe"?

Finally, in his concluding sentence of Jesus' death scene, John leaves us with this last thought: "They will look on the one whom they have pierced" (19:37). Was it John's intent to have us understand that the image of the pierced man of the shroud that we all look upon today is the fulfillment of this Scripture?

Even if John were attempting to describe the shroud image and its blood marks, what is it about this image that John describes in chapter 19 that should convince his readers, first-century Jews, to believe that Jesus is the Son of God? Is it only the fact that these events were predicted in Scripture, or is there another factor not yet made explicit that would bring his readers to "believe"?

Notes and References

Chapter One
DR. BARBET: THE PHYSICIAN DETECTIVE

1. Pierre Barbet, *A Doctor at Calvary* (New York: Doubleday and Co., Inc., 1953).
2. In 1983, the House of Savoy willed the shroud to the Roman Catholic Church. The shroud remains in Turin Cathedral where it has been kept since 1578.
3. Barbet, 6–7.
4. Ian Wilson, *The Shroud of Turin* (New York: Doubleday and Co., Inc., 1978), 13–14.
5. Barbet, 17.
6. Ibid., 17.
7. Ibid., 31.
8. Ibid., 17.
9. Ibid., 91. Multiple facial wounds described by Barbet.
10. Ibid., 92.
11. Ibid., 92.
12. Ibid., 93–97.
13. Ibid., 129–147.
14. Ibid., 121–128.
15. Ibid., 148–152.

16. Ibid., 107.
17. Ibid., 103 and 124. There are some early examples of art forms showing the nail through the wrist. The most famous is the Gero Crucifix of Cologne from the tenth century. (Personal communication with Dorothy Crispino.)
18. Ibid., 110–112.
19. Ibid., 118.
20. Ibid., 119.

Chapter Two
TURIN: BECOMING PARTICIPANTS

1. Pierre Barbet, *A Doctor at Calvary* (New York: Doubleday and Co., 1953), 8.
2. Ibid., 32.

Chapter Three
TURIN: SCIENCE AND THE SHROUD

1. Max Frei, "Nine Years of Palinological Studies on the Shroud," *Shroud Spectrum International* (June 1982): 3. (English spelling is Palynological.)
2. Ibid., 5.
3. Ibid., 5–7.
4. Ibid., 7.
5. Ian Wilson, *The Shroud of Turin* (New York: Doubleday and Co., Inc., 1978), 116.
6. Edward Gibbon, *The Decline and Fall of the Roman Empire,* vol. II (Chicago: Encyclopedia Britannica, Inc., 1952), 196–197.
7. Wilson, 135.
8. Ibid., 145.

9. Ibid., 147.

10. Ibid., 145–147.

11. Ibid., chapter 20, 165–183.

12. John Jackson, Eric Jumper, and William Ercoline, "Correlation of Image Intensity on the Turin Shroud with the 3-D Structure of a Human Body Shape," *Applied Optics* vol. 23 (July 15, 1984): 2247.

13. Ibid., 2249.

14. Among the outstanding American scientific literature that is presently available on the shroud are the following, which are very technical:

   a. L.A. Schwalbe and R.N. Rogers, "Physics and Chemistry of the Shroud of Turin: A Summary of the 1978 Investigation," *Analytica Chimica Acta,* vol. 135 (1982): 3–49.

   b. J.H. Heller and A.D. Adler, "A Chemical Investigation of the Shroud of Turin," *Canadian Society of Forensic Science Journal,* vol. 14, no. 3 (1981): 81–103.

   c. V.D. Miller and S.F. Pellicori, "Ultraviolet Fluorescence Photography of the Shroud of Turin," *Journal of Biological Photography,* vol. 49, no. 3 (July 1981): 71–85.

   d. S.F. Pellicori and R.A. Chandos, "Portable Unit Permits UV/Vis Study of Shroud," *Industrial Research and Development* (February 1981): 186–189.

   e. R.A. Morris, L.A. Schwalbe, and J.R. London, "X-Ray Fluorescence Investigation of the Shroud of Turin," *X-Ray Spectrometry,* vol 9, no. 2 (1980): 40–47.

   f. J.H. Heller and A.D. Adler, "Blood on the Shroud of Turin," *Applied Optics,* vol. 19, no. 16 (August 15, 1980): 2742–2744.

g. E.J. Jumper and R.W. Mottern, "Scientific Investigation of the Shroud of Turin," *Applied Optics* (June 15, 1980): 1909–1912.

h. S.F. Pellicori, "Spectral Properties of the Shroud of Turin," *Applied Optics* (June 15, 1980): 1913–1920.

i. J.S. Accetta and J.S. Baumgart, "Infrared Reflectance Spectroscopy and Thermographic Investigations of the Shroud of Turin," *Applied Optics* (June 15, 1980): 1921–1929.

j. Roger Gilbert and Marion Gilbert, "Ultraviolet-Visible Reflectance and Fluorescence Spectra of the Shroud of Turin," *Applied Optics* (June 15, 1980): 1930–1936.

k. R.W. Mottern, R.J. London, and R.A. Morris, "Radiographic Examination of the Shroud of Turin—A Preliminary Report," *Materials Evaluation,* vol. 38, no. 12 (1979): 39–44.

l. V. Miller and D. Lynn, "De Lijkwada Van Turijn," *Natuur en Techniek* (February 1981): 102–125.

m. Robert Bucklin, "The Shroud of Turin: A Pathologist's Viewpoint," *Legal Medicine Annual* (1981).

n. S. Pellicori and M. Evans, "The Shroud of Turin Through the Microscope," *Archaeology* (January–February 1981): 32–42.

15. Schwalbe and Rogers, "Physics and Chemistry of the Shroud of Turin," op. cit., 31. "There has been no evidence found to suggest that the visible image results from a colored foreign material on the cloth. In this regard, the data are quite internally consistent. Microscopic studies have revealed the image to be highly superficial; the image resides in the topmost fibers of the woven material as a translucent yellow discoloration. No pigment particles can be resolved by direct Shroud observation at 50x magnification, nor can

unambiguously identified pigment particles be found on the tape samples at 1,000x. Microchemical studies of yellow fibrils taken from tape samples of the pure-image area have shown no indication for the presence of dyes, stains, inorganic pigments, or protein-, starch-, or wax-based painting media. X-ray fluorescence shows no detectable difference in elemental composition between image and non-image areas. Spectrophotometric reflectance reveals none of the characteristic spectral features of pigments or dyes. Ultraviolet fluorescence shows no indication of aromatic dyes or aromatic amino acids that might be expected from animal-collagen pigment binders. Direct visual observations of image areas that intersect scorch and water stains reveal nothing that might suggest the presence of organic dyes or water- protein-, or starch-based painting media."

16. McCrone's four articles:
    a. Walter C. McCrone and C. Skirius, "Light Microscopical Study of the Turin 'Shroud' I," *The Microscope,* vol. 28, no. 3 (1980): 105–113.
    b. Walter C. McCrone, "Light Microscopical Study of the Turin 'Shroud' II," *The Microscope,* vol. 28, no. 4 (1980): 115–128.
    c. Walter C. McCrone, "Microscopical Study of the Turin 'Shroud' III," *The Microscope,* vol. 29 (1981): 19–39.
    d. Walter C. McCrone, "The Shroud of Turin: Blood or Artist's Pigment?" *Accounts of Chemical Research,* vol. 23, no. 3 (1990): 77–87.

17. Scientific reviews of McCrone's articles:
    a. Pellicori and Evans, "The Shroud of Turin through the Microscope," op. cit., 42.
    b. Schwalbe and Rogers, "Physics and Chemistry of the Shroud of Turin," op. cit., 11–16.

c. Jackson, Jumper, and Ercoline, "Correlation of Image Intensity on the Turin Shroud with the 3-D Structure of a Human Body Shape," op. cit., 2251–2253.

d. Eric Jumper, Alan Adler, John Jackson, Samuel Pellicori, John Heller, and James Druzik, "A Comprehensive Examination of the Various Stains and Images on the Shroud of Turin," *Archaeological Chemistry III*, edited by J. Lambert, ACS Advances in Chemistry, no. 205 (1984): 447–476.

e. Heller and Adler, "A Chemical Investigation of the Shroud of Turin," op. cit., 81–103.

f. Personal communication from Jumper and Adler concerning article "17-d," p. 468: "Under the experimental conditions employed in the x-ray investigation on the shroud, unfortunately iron would not be expected to show images as was implied in the review article. However, vermilion (mercuric sulfide, HgS) would be seen."

g. For the reader who is scientifically inclined, I would suggest carefully reading McCrone's article "16-d," Adler's article "17-e," and Jumper's article "17-d" so that you may decide for yourself, at the microscopic and chemical level, whether or not the shroud is a painting. To fully comprehend McCrone's article, you need to review the colored pictures in his article.

18. Heller and Adler, "Blood on the Shroud of Turin," op. cit., 2742. For those interested in reading more about the blood on the shroud, I suggest reading the work of Pierluigi Baima Bollone. His own bibliography is in his *Shroud Spectrum International* articles. See bibliography.

19. Heller and Adler, "A Chemical Investigation of the Shroud of Turin," op. cit., 81.

20. Among Adler's best articles are the following:
    a. Heller and Adler, "A Chemical Investigation of the Shroud of Turin," op. cit.
    b. Heller and Adler, "Blood on the Shroud of Turin," op. cit.
    c. Jumper, Adler, et al., "A Comprehensive Examination of the Various Stains and Images on the Shroud of Turin," op. cit.
21. Schwalbe and Rogers, "Physics and Chemistry of the Shroud of Turin," op. cit., 36.
22. Pellicori and Evans, "The Shroud of Turin through the Microscope," op. cit., 41.
23. Schwalbe and Rogers, "Physics and Chemistry of the Shroud of Turin," op. cit., 11.
24. Heller and Adler, "A Chemical Investigation of the Shroud of Turin," op. cit., 81. "There is no chemical evidence for the application of any pigments, stains, or dyes on the cloth to produce the image found thereon. The chemical differences between image and non-image areas of the cloth indicate that the image was produced by some dehydrative oxidative process of the cellulose structure of the linen to yield a conjugated carbonyl group as the chromophore. However, a detailed mechanism for the production of this image, accounting for all of its properties, remains undetermined."
25. Articles describing the use of substances to produce yellowing of fibers are the following:
    a. Heller and Adler, "A Chemical Investigation of the Shroud of Turin," op. cit., 98–99.
    b. Pellicori, "Spectral Properties of the Shroud of Turin," op. cit., 1913–1920.
26. Four of the best articles describing the problems of the contact theory are the following:

a. Schwalbe and Rogers, "Physics and Chemistry of the Shroud of Turin," op. cit., 35. "If the image had been caused by the catalytic action of materials present on the corpse, direct contact of the body with the cloth seems to be the only likely material transfer mechanism. A general problem now becomes apparent. It would seem to follow that the dorsal image area was influenced by the weight of the body whereas the frontal image was imprinted only by the lesser weight of the covering cloth. Recall, however, that the densities at presumed contact points on both frontal and dorsal images do not differ significantly. These characteristics along with the superficial nature of the image would suggest that the contact transfer mechanism is pressure-independent. This apparent contradiction challenges not only the Pellicori-German model but most other hypotheses in this category."

b. Pellicori and Evans, "The Shroud of Turin through the Microscope," op. cit., 43.

c. Heller and Adler, "A Chemical Investigation of the Shroud of Turin," op. cit., 98–99

d. Jumper, Adler, et. al., "A Comprehensive Examination of the Various Stains and Images on the Shroud of Turin," op. cit., 470. "The Shroud's mapping relationship, however, poses the strongest objection to a contact mechanism. Contact mechanisms have not been able to produce a convincing cloth-body distance relationship. In fact, taken alone, this mapping function seems to suggest some kind of a "projection" mechanism, because there seems to be image present even where it does not appear to have been possible that the cloth was in contact with the body. We are left to identify what kind of 'projection' mechanism, and this we have been unable to do. Simple molecular diffusion and 'radiation' models, for example, fail to account for the apparent resolution of the image as we understand it."

27. Jackson, Jumper, and Ercoline, "Correlation of Image Intensity on the Turin Shroud with the 3-D Structure of a Human Body Shape" op. cit., 2244–2270.

28. No mechanism is known that will reproduce the body-to-cloth transfer. The following articles discuss this:
   a. Ibid.
   b. Schwalbe and Rogers, "Physics and Chemistry of the Shroud of Turin," op.cit., 35.
   c. Heller and Adler, "A Chemical Investigation of the Shroud of Turin," op. cit., 99.

29. Jumper, Adler, et. al., "A Comprehensive Examination of the Various Stains and Images on the Shroud of Turin," op. cit., 460.

30. Ibid., 447–476.

31. Ibid., 450–451, and verbal communication with Jumper regarding wicking.

32. Ibid., 450 and 459.

33. Pellicori and Evans, "The Shroud of Turin through the Microscope," op. cit., 41. (*Personal communication with Jumper:* The image fibers penetrated the thread one fiber deep and possibly in some places, two fibers deep, even though it says three to four fibers deep on page 41 of Pellicori's article.)

34. Jumper, Adler, et. al., "A Comprehensive Examination of the Various Stains and Images on the Shroud of Turin," op. cit., 451.

Chapter Four
JEWISH BURIAL CUSTOMS

1. *The Mishnah,* translated by Herbert Danby. (Oxford: Oxford University Press, 1933), Second Division, Moed. Tractate: Shabbath, 23⁵, 120.

2. Maurice Lamm, *The Jewish Way in Death and Mourning* (New York: Jonathan David, Publishers, 1969), 6–7.

3. Ibid., 244.

4. Solomon Ganzfried, *Code of Jewish Law (Kitzur Shulchan Aruch),* translated by Hyman E. Goldin (New York: Hebrew Publishing Company, 1963) vol. IV, ch. 197. *The Purification, Shrouds, and Utilization of Anything Belonging to the Dead* (Tahara), nos. 9 and 10, 99–100.

5. *The Mishnah,* op.cit., Introduction, XIII.

6. *The Mishnah,* op.cit., Third Division, Nashim. Tractate: Nazir, 7², 289–290.

7. Ibid., Sixth Division, Tohoroth. Tractate: Oholoth, 3⁵, 653–654.

8. Ibid., Appendix II: Money, Weights, and Measures, 798.

9. Ibid., Third Division, Nashim. Tractate: Nazir, 7², 290.

10. Ganzfried, *Code of Jewish Law,* op. cit., 99.

11. Ibid., 100.

12. *The Mishnah,* op.cit., Fifth Division, Kodashim. Tractate: Zebahim, 3¹, note. 4, 471.

13. Bonnie Lavoie, Gilbert Lavoie, Daniel Klutstein, and John Regan, "In Accordance with Jewish Burial Custom, the Body of Jesus Was Not Washed," *Sindon* (December 1981): 19–29. Also in *Shroud Spectrum International* (June 1982): 8–17 and *Biblical Archeologist,* "Polemics and Irenics" (Winter 1981): 5–6.

Chapter Five
BLOOD OFF THE LEFT ELBOW

1. *The Mishnah,* translated by Herbert Danby. (Oxford: Oxford University Press, 1933), Sixth Division, Tohoroth, Tractate: Oholoth, 3^5, 654.
2. Gilbert Lavoie, Bonnie Lavoie, Vincent Donovan, and John Ballas, "Blood on the Shroud of Turin: Part I," *Shroud Spectrum International* (June 1983): 15–19.

Chapter Six
THE TRANSFER OF BLOOD CLOTS TO CLOTH

1. Gilbert Lavoie, Bonnie Lavoie, Vincent Donovan, and John Ballas, "Blood on the Shroud of Turin: Part II," *Shroud Spectrum International,* no. 8 (1983): 2–10.
2. Clara Davidsohn and Minnie Wells, Todd-Sanford Clinical Diagnosis by Laboratory Methods. Philadelphia: W.B. Saunders Co. (1962): 346.
3. Ibid., 332.
4. Ibid., 330.
5. I placed three drops of normal saline on all of the clots fifteen minutes prior to each of the half-hour sample times throughout the four-hour period. However, once the cloth was placed on a clot, no further saline was placed on that clot.
6. Pierre Barbet, *A Doctor at Calvary* (New York: Doubleday and Co. Inc., 1953, Appendix I.) According to Barbet's description of the death of a man hung by his arms, profuse sweat pours from the body just prior to the time of death.
7. *The Mishnah,* translated by Herbert Danby. (Oxford: Oxford University Press, 1933), Second Division, Moed. Tractate: Shabbath, 23^5, 120.

8. The 1995 Israeli Calendar, published by the Government Press Office, Jerusalem, Israel, obtained from the Israeli Consulate, Boston, Massachusetts.
9. Vern Miller and S. F. Pellicori, "Ultraviolet Fluorescence Photography of the Shroud of Turin," *Journal of Biological Photography*, vol. 49, no. 3 (July 1981): 75.
10. Ibid., 82.
11. J.H. Heller and A.D. Adler, "A Chemical Investigation of the Shroud of Turin," *Canadian Society of Forensic Science Journal*, vol. 14, no. 3 (1981): 96.
12. *The Mishnah,* op. cit., Sixth Division, Tohoroth. Tractate: Oholoth, 3^5, 653–654.
13. Barbet, op. cit., 24–25.

Chapter Seven
BLOOD ON THE FACE

1. Pierre Barbet, *A Doctor at Calvary* (New York: Doubleday and Co., Inc., 1953): 32.
2. Eric Jumper, Alan Adler, John Jackson, Samuel Pellicori, John Heller, and James Druzik, "A Comprehensive Examination of the Various Stains and Images on the Shroud of Turin," *Archaeological Chemistry* III, ACS Advances in Chemistry, edited by J. Lambert, no. 205 (1984): 470 and 474.
3. Gilbert Lavoie, Bonnie Lavoie, and Alan Adler, "Blood on the Shroud of Turin: Part III, The Blood on the Face," *Shroud Spectrum International* (September 1986): 3–6.

Chapter Eight
CARBON DATING THE SHROUD

1. P.E. Damon, D.J. Donahue, B.H. Gore, et. al., "Radiocarbon Dating of the Shroud of Turin," *Nature,* vol. 337 (February 16, 1989): 611–615.

2. H.E. Gove, "Progress in Radiocarbon Dating the Shroud of Turin," *Radiocarbon,* vol. 31, no. 3 (1989): 965–969.

3. H.E. Gove, "Dating the Turin Shroud—An Assessment," *Radiocarbon,* vol. 32, no. 1 (1990): 87–92.

4. Eric Jumper, Alan Adler, John Jackson, Samuel Pellicori, John Heller, and James Druzik, "A Comprehensive Examination of the Various Stains and Images on the Shroud of Turin," *Archaeological Chemistry* III, ACS Advances in Chemistry, edited by J. Lambert, no. 205 (1984): 474.

5. New information on radiocarbon dating:
   a. G. Harbottle and W. Heino, "Carbon Dating the Shroud of Turin," *Archaeological Chemistry-IV:* Allen, R. O., ed.: Advances in Chemistry, no. 220; American Chemical Society (1989): 313–320.
   b. A.D. Adler, "Updating Recent Studies on the Shroud of Turin," *Archaeological Chemistry:* Orna, M. V., ed.: ACS Symposium Series, no. 625 (1996): 223–228.
   c. M.V. Orna, "Doing Chemistry at the Art/Archaeology Interface," *Journal of Chemical Education,* vol. 74, no.3 (April 1997): 373–376.

6. Harbottle, 318–319.

7. Adler, 225.

8. Harbottle, 316.

9. Adler, 225.

10. Orna, 375.

11. For further discussion, these references are recommended:
    a. Harbottle, 313–320.

b. Adler, 223–228.

c. Orna, 373–376.

Chapter Nine
THE SHADOWS OF THE IMAGE

1. Personal communication with Alan Adler—He states that the lower backside appears flattened per the VP8 image analyser. In rechecking this area, I also noted that the scourge marks at the middle area of the lower backside, especially toward the right (Figure 13 of Chapter 9), do suggest the possibility of a flattened lower backside. (The flatness of a body part can be best appreciated by placing the calf of one's leg on a glass table and observing the flatness from under the table. However, the type of flattening that is seen in the autopsy room, caused by the subject lying on a hard surface, continues to persist even after the body is lifted up from a hard surface table.)

   The observation of a possible partial flattening of the lower backside of the shroud image would be consistent with the corpse having been laid in the supine position on a hard surface. This observation is the logical consequence of other findings: chest wound, scourged body, wounds of crucifixion—all contributing causes leading to death. However, among these findings are the shadows under the lower backside (see Figure 1C of Chapter 1) and under the hair (compare Figure 10 to 11B of Chapter 9) as well as the flow of hair down to the shoulders and upper back. These observations are consistent with an image of an upright man.

2. The hair of the shroud image is three dimensional by VP8 image analysis. The VP8 also demonstates a three-dimensional image of Reverend John Arens' whitened hair; his

dark hair does not show a three-dimensional image. (Unpublished VP8 Image Study done by G.R. Lavoie, M.D. and Kevin Moran.)

3. The contents of chapter 9 were presented at the 1989 Paris International Shroud Symposium. (Unpublished paper.)

Chapter Ten
JOSEPHUS: THE IMAGE OF A MAN

1. Personal communication with Rev. Stephen E. Salocks, S.S.L., Professor of the New Testament, St. John's Seminary.
2. Flavius Josephus, *The Life and Works of Flavius Josephus.* (Philadelphia: David McKay Co., no date, translated by William Whiston) "Wars of the Jews," Book II, chapter X, 1, 3, and 4, 678–679. (Boldface added by author for emphasis.)
3. *The Mishnah,* translated by Herbert Danby. (Oxford: Oxford University Press, 1933), Fourth Division, Nezikin. Tractate: Abodah Zarah 3[1], 440.

Chapter Eleven
THE FOURTH GOSPEL

1. There is discussion among biblical scholars as to the authorship of the letters of John. See: *The New Oxford Annotated Bible* (copyright 1991), page 349 NT. Nevertheless, it is clear that in the Johannine literature there is a consistent pattern regarding secrecy. (Personal communication with Walter Abbott, S.J., scripture scholar.)
2. Even though John does not mention a linen cloth (shroud) among the burial cloths, he previously acknowledged it when he stated that Jesus was buried "according to the burial

custom of the Jews" (John 19:40). For further discussion see Chapter 4. Moreover, the Synoptic Gospels confirm that it was the custom to use a linen cloth (shroud) in a burial such as Jesus': Matthew 27:59, Mark 15:46, and Luke 23:53. For further discussion of the burial cloths, see: John A.T. Robinson, "The Shroud and the New Testament," *Face to Face with the Turin Shroud,* ed. Peter Jennings (Oxford England: Mowbray and Co., Inc., 1978), 69–80.

3. Raymond Brown, *The Gospel According to John,* vol. 29 (I–XII) and vol. 29A (XIII–XXI) (New York: Doubleday and Co., Inc., 1970), 1046.

4. Flavius Josephus, *The Life and Works of Flavius Josephus.* (Philadelphia: David McKay Co., no date, translated by William Whiston), "Wars of the Jews," Book II, chapter X, 1, 3, and 4, 678–679.

5. During the time of Jesus, something not made by human hands was recognized as coming from God: "We heard him say, 'I will destroy this temple that is made with hands, and in three days I will build another, not made with hands'" (Mark 14:58).

6. The commentators concern themselves with all the possible sources of each narrative in John's gospel. However, regardless of the sources, when one considers that John's gospel was shaped by *one principal disciple* (see asterisk, page 143), then is it not reasonable that this disciple would have used his gathered sources in such a way as to communicate his intended message?

What was John's intent when he created for his readers a mystery that has caused biblical commentators to ask over and over again the very same questions? What was it in the tomb that caused John to believe? Was it the position of the cloths? What was the object of the verb *saw?* Why does John 20:8 present a statement that conflicts with John 20:9: "For as yet they did not understand the scripture, that he must rise from the dead"? (Schnackenburg and others ask this last question. See bibliography.) In another scene, both Brown and Schnackenburg ask why Mary Magdalene does not see the burial cloths when she looks into the tomb. Why is it that the answers to these questions are all logically explained once the shroud with its image is placed in the tomb? Has not John accomplished his intended goal?

Chapter Twelve
THE VISION OF DANIEL

1. The more I thought of the white-haired man of the shroud the more I wondered. Over time I came across the following biblical verses that caused me to contemplate the possibility that the white-haired man of the shroud carries a profound theological message:

> *"As I watched, thrones were set in place, and an Ancient One took his throne, his clothing was white as snow, and the hair of his head like pure wool."*
> *Daniel 7:9*

> *Philip said to him, "Lord, show us the Father, and we will be satisfied." Jesus said to him, "Have I been with you all this time, Philip, and you still do not know me? Whoever has seen me has seen the Father. How can you say, 'Show us the Father'? Do you not believe that I am in the Father and the Father is in me? The words that I say to you I do not speak on my own; but the Father who dwells in me does his works. Believe me that I am in the Father and the Father is in me; but if you do not, then believe me because of the works themselves.*
> *John 14:8–11*

He is the image of the invisible God.
                                    Colossians 1:15

I leave it to the readers to draw their own conclusions and suggest to those who may have further interest in this discussion to read the fine work of Christoph Schönborn, O.P., *God's Human Face* (Ignatius Press, San Francisco, 1994).

2. Raymond Brown, *The Gospel According to John,* vol. 29 (I–XII) and vol. 29A (XIII–XXI) (New York: Doubleday and Co., Inc., 1986), CXV in introduction.

3. Ibid., 146.

4. *The New Oxford Annotated Bible* (copyright 1991) gives "one like a human being." Footnote (a) for this verse notes that the Aramaic is "one like a son of man." In future reference to this chapter and verse I will use the Aramaic. Daniel 7:13–14 was taken from the *NOAB* rather than the *Jerusalem Bible* simply for the sake of continuity.

5. *Daniel. The ArtScroll Tanach Series* (Brooklyn, New York: Mesorah Publications, Ltd., 1980), 206. Rashi is an acronym for Rabbi Shlomo ben Yetzchak, 1040–1105.

6. Levi Khamor, *The Revelation of the Son of Man* (Massachusetts: St. Bede's Publications, 1989), 130–131. "The 'Son of Man' who came with 'the clouds of heaven' in Daniel 7:13–14 was none other than the Messiah according to the rabbis (see Midrash on Psalms 2.9; 21.5; Midrash Numbers Rabbah 13.14; Midrash Haggadol re Genesis 41:1; Tanchumah on Genesis 27:30–32; Yalkut Shimoni fol. 571; Tanchumah Toledoth 20.4; Sanhedrin 38b; 98a, Babylonian Talmud; Seder Rab Amran [Sepher Hechaloth] i.13a in Jellinek's *Beth haMidrash* vol. V, p. 168; VI, pp. 150 ff.; Rashi and Saadia Gaon *ad loc.;* see also Rabbi S. Cohen's, *La Bible,* vol. 17, p. 38, and Rabbi Z. Kahn's, *Bible Rabbinique,* vol. 2, p. 492, n. 4 re Daniel 7:13 Messianically interpreted). In the Judaica section of the British Museum Library there is an

old Hebrew manuscript (MS. 1048–Harley 5686) which states in folio 128a: 'These are the glad tidings of the Messiah ben David, that is, the Son of Man.'"

7. "And remember, I am with you always, to the end of the age" (Matthew 28:20).

8. In any discussion of the Son of Man and the last days, reference is always made to Daniel, chapter 7. (See comment on Matthew 24:30 in *The New Oxford Annotated Bible*, 1991.) However, as is evident, the focus of this study is not on the last days.

Appendix A

1. Gilbert R. Lavoie, "The Difference in the Length of the Arms Is an Optical Illusion," *Shroud Spectrum International* (March 1989): 3–7.

Appendix B

1. From a medical point of view, the source of the blood could have been from the large vessels of the chest or from the heart. The source of the water could have been from pleural fluid (that can look like water), which accumulated in the chest cavity. The causes of fluid accumulation in the chest are numerous. A plausible cause may have been congestive heart failure, which could have resulted from shock (blood and fluid loss, causing a profound drop in blood pressure leading to death). No one can know the exact mechanisms of the occurrence but the flow of "blood and water" is certainly medically possible.

On the back image of the shroud, along the waist, there is a large liquidlike flow (Figure 1). This flow consists of several streams of what appears to be bloody fluid (blood mixed with a lighter clearer fluid) that flow beyond the perimeter of the body image. The blood marks that reach beyond the body image are located below the paralleling patches where the burns occurred during the fire of 1532. The water marks that quenched the smoldering linen at that time are located around the patches and intermingle with the blood marks. These water marks seen on each side of the body are surrounded by a very light line that determines their perimeters.* On close observation of the streams at the small of the back (Figure 1), there are light, nearly colorless areas of fluid interspersed between the darker areas of blood, reminiscent of the flow of "blood and water" described by John.

Again, like the flow of "blood and water," no one knows the specific circumstances causing the flow across the lower back, but some reasonable assumptions as to the major events leading up to this formation can be made. Very likely, this flow of bloody fluid came from the open side-wound after the body was taken down from the vertical position of crucifixion and placed on the shroud in the horizontal position in preparation for burial. The blood and fluid flowed down the side of the chest onto the shroud. It then flowed behind the small of the back and across to the opposite side of the back and beyond. (Years ago, a similar flow of fluid from the chest to the back was reproduced by Vernon Miller and his team. *Verbal communication with Vernon Miller.*)

When considering the blood marks of the shroud, John's description of Jesus' death is exact, even down to the detail

---

* The water marks are better seen in Figure 2 where the gray area has been added for clarity. The outer perimeters on the gray zones in Figure 2 demonstrate the outer perimeter of the water marks. When looking at Vern Miller's full-size high resolution colored photograph, one can more easily distinguish between the blood and the lighter clearer fluid, the water marks, and the burn marks. (Technical support for this study supplied by Kevin Moran and Andre Lavoie.)

Figure 1

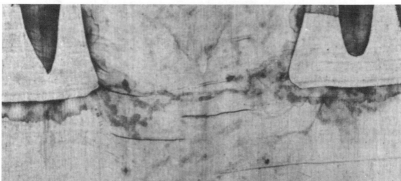

Figure 2

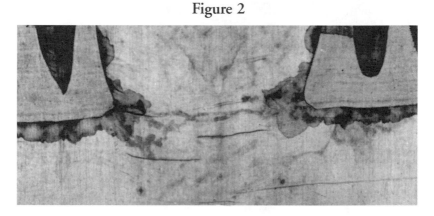

of the flow of "blood and water." Indeed, with the shroud in hand, there is no doubt of John's accuracy: "His testimony is true, and he knows that he tells the truth" (19:35).

Over the centuries, theologians have searched for the clearest and most relevant theological meaning to John's emphatic eyewitness report. Brown continues in this tradition: "Thus we have every reason to search for a profound theological symbolism in the flow of blood and water." (See reference note 1 of chapter 11, p. 949 in Brown's book.) Brown beautifully reviews the theological symbolism of the past and proposes other theological symbolic references which he finds in John's gospel and in 1 John (pp. 944–956 in Brown's book). Brown comments that 1 John and John "share in common the themes of water and blood, the Spirit, and testimony" (p. 950 in Brown's book). I also suspect that they share in common the water and blood, the image, and the testimony of the shroud.

2. *The New Oxford Annotated Bible*, (New York: Oxford University Press, 1991), John 19:36. Jesus fulfills the Passover (Exodus 12: 46). John 19:37: (Zechariah 12:10). For an in-depth study of the meaning of these scriptures, I would suggest reading the commentary of Raymond E. Brown, 944–956. (See reference note 1 of chapter 11.)

Bibliography

———— ⚮ ••• ⚮ ————

Accetta, J. and J.S. Baumgart. "Infrared Reflectance Spectroscopy and Thermographic Investigations of the Shroud of Turin." *Applied Optics* (June 15, 1980): 1921–1929.

Adler, Alan. "Updating Recent Studies on the Shroud of Turin." *Archaeological Chemistry:* M. V. Orna, ed., ACS Symposium Series, no. 625 (1996): 223–228.

Barbet, Pierre. *A Doctor at Calvary.* New York: Doubleday and Co., Inc., 1953.

Beasley-Murray, George R. *Word Biblical Commentary.* Volume II. John. Waco, Texas: Word Books, 1987.

Bollone, Pierluigi Baima, M. Jorio, and A.L. Massaro. "Identification of the Group of the Traces of Human Blood on the Shroud." *Shroud Spectrum International.* (March 1983): 3–6.

Bollone, Pierluigi Baima, and Agostino Gaglio. "Demonstration of Blood, Aloes, and Myrrh on the Holy Shroud with Immunofluorescence Techniques." *Shroud Spectrum International* (December 1984): 3–8.

Brown, Raymond. *The Gospel According to John.* New York: Doubleday and Co., Inc., 1970.

Brown, Raymond E. *The Community of the Beloved Disciple.* New York: Paulist Press, 1979.

Bucklin, Robert. "The Shroud of Turin: A Pathologist's Viewpoint." *Legal Medicine Annual,* 1981.

Damon, P E., D.J. Donahue, B.H. Gore, A.L. Hatheway, A.J. Jull, T. W. Linick, P.J. Sercel, L.J. Toolin, C.R. Bronk, E.T. Hall, et. al. "Radiocarbon Dating of the Shroud of Turin." *Nature,* vol. 337 (February 16, 1989): 611–615.

Daniel. The ArtScroll Tanach Series. Brooklyn, New York: Mesorah Publications, Ltd., 1980.

Davidsohn, Clara and Minnie Well. *Todd-Sanford Clinical Diagnosis by Laboratory Methods.* Philadelphia: W. B. Saunders Co., 1962.

Frei, Max. "Nine Years of Palinological Studies on the Shroud." *Shroud Spectrum International.* Nashville, Indiana: Indiana Center for Shroud Studies (June 1982): 3–7. (English spelling is Palynological.)

Ganzfried, Solomon. *Code of Jewish Law (Kitzur Shulchan Aruch).* Translated by Hyman E. Goldin. New York: Hebrew Publishing Co., 1963.

Gibbon, Edward. *The Decline and Fall of the Roman Empire.* Volume II. Chicago: Encyclopedia Britannica, Inc., 1952.

Gilbert, Roger, and Marion Gilbert. "Ultraviolet-Visible Reflectance and Fluorescence Spectra of the Shroud of Turin." *Applied Optics* (June 15, 1980): 1930–1936.

Gove, H.E. "Dating the Turin Shroud—An Assessment." *Radiocarbon,* vol. 32, no. 1 (1990): 87–92.

Gove, H.E. "Progress in Radiocarbon Dating the Shroud of Turin." *Radiocarbon,* vol. 31, no. 3 (1989): 965–969.

Harbottle, German, and Walden Heino. "Carbon Dating the Shroud of Turin," *Archaeological Chemistry-IV:* R. O. Allen, ed., ACS Advances in Chemistry, no. 220 (1989): 313–320.

Heller, John and Alan Adler. "Blood on the Shroud of Turin." *Applied Optics* (August 15, 1980): 2742–2744.

Heller, J. and Adler, A. "A Chemical Investigation of the Shroud of Turin." *Canadian Society of Forensic Science Journal,* vol. 14, no. 3 (1981): 81–103.

Israeli Calendar, 1995. Published by the Government Press Office, Jerusalem, Israel. Obtained from the Israeli Consulate, Boston, Massachusetts.

Jackson, John, Eric Jumper, and William Ercoline. "Correlation of Image Intensity on the Turin Shroud with the 3-D Structure of a Human Body Shape." *Applied Optics* (July 15, 1984): 2244–2270.

Jennings, Peter, ed. *Face to Face with the Turin Shroud.* Oxford England: Mowbray and Co., Inc., 1978.

Jerusalem Bible. London: Darton, Longman, and Todd, 1966.

Josephus, Flavius. *The Life and Works of Flavius Josephus*. Translated by William Whiston (1667–1752). "Wars of the Jews," Book II, chapter X. Philadelphia: David McKay Company, (no date).

Jumper, Eric, and Robert Mottern. "Scientific Investigation of the Shroud of Turin." *Applied Optics* (June 15, 1980):1909–1912.

Jumper, Eric, Alan Adler, John Jackson, Samuel Pellicori, John Heller, and James Druzik. "A Comprehensive Examination of the Various Stains and Images on the Shroud of Turin," *Archaeological Chemistry* III, J. Lambert, ed., ACS Advances in Chemistry, no. 205 (1984): 447–476.

Khamor, Levi. *The Revelation of the Son of Man*. Massachusetts: St. Bede's Publications, 1989.

Lamm, Maurice. *The Jewish Way in Death and Mourning*. New York: Jonathan David, Publishers, 1969.

Lavoie, Gilbert R. "The Difference in the Length of the Arms Is an Optical Illusion." *Shroud Spectrum International* (March 1989): 3–7.

Lavoie, Gilbert R., Bonnie B. Lavoie, Vincent Donovan, and John Ballas. "Blood on the Shroud of Turin: Part I." *Shroud Spectrum International* (June 1983): 15–19.

———. "Blood on the Shroud of Turin: Part II." *Shroud Spectrum International* (September 1983): 2–10.

Lavoie, Gilbert R., Bonnie B. Lavoie, and Alan Adler. "Blood on the Shroud of Turin: Part III: The Blood on the Face." *Shroud Spectrum International* (September 1986): 3–6.

Lavoie, Gilbert R., Bonnie B. Lavoie, Daniel Klutstein, and John Regan. "In Accordance with Jewish Burial Custom, The Body of Jesus Was Not Washed." *Shroud Spectrum International* (June 1982): 8–17.

———. "The Body of Jesus Was Not Washed According to the Jewish Burial Custom." *Sindon*. (December 1981): 19–29.

———. "Jesus, the Turin Shroud, and Jewish Burial Customs." *Biblical Archeologist* (Winter 1982): 5–6.

McCrone, W., and C. Skirius. "Light Microscopical Study of the Turin 'Shroud' I." *The Microscope*, vol. 28, no. 3 (1980): 105–113.

McCrone, W. "Light Microscopical Study of the Turin 'Shroud' II." *The Microscope*, vol. 28, no. 4 (1980): 115–128.

———. "Microscopical Study of the Turin 'Shroud' III." *The Microscope*, vol. 29, (1981): 19–38.

————. "The Shroud of Turin: Blood or Artist's Pigment?" *Accounts of Chemical Research*, vol. 23, no. 3 (1990): 77–87.

Miller, Vern, and D. Lynn. "De Lijkwada Van Turijn." *Natuur en Techniek* (February 1981): 102–125.

Miller, Vern, and Samuel Pellicori. "Ultraviolet Fluorescence Photography of the Shroud of Turin." *Journal of Biological Photography*, vol. 49, no. 3 (July 1981): 71–85.

The Mishnah. Translated by Herbert Danby. Oxford: Oxford University Press, 1933.

Morris, R., L. Schwalbe, and J. London. "X-Ray Fluorescence Investigation of the Shroud of Turin." *X-Ray Spectrometry*, vol. 5, no. 2 (1980): 40–47.

Mottern, R.W., R.J. London, and R.A. Morris. "Radiographic Examination of the Shroud of Turin—A Preliminary Report." *Materials Evaluation*, vol. 38, no. 12 (1979): 39–44.

The New Oxford Annotated Bible. New York: Oxford University Press, 1991.

Orna, Mary Virginia. "Doing Chemistry at the Art/Archaeology Interface." *Journal of Chemical Education*, vol. 74, no. 4 (April 1997): 373–376.

Pellicori, Samuel. "Spectral Properties of the Shroud of Turin." *Applied Optics* (June 15, 1980): 1913–1920.

Pellicori, Samuel, and R. Chandos. "Portable Unit Permits UV/Vis Study of Shroud." *Industrial Research and Development* (February 1981): 186–189.

Pellicori, Samuel, and Mark Evans. "The Shroud of Turin through the Microscope." *Archeology* (January-February 1981): 32–42.

Schönborn, O.P., Christoph. *God's Human Face.* San Francisco: Ignatius Press, 1994.

Schnackenburg, Rudolf. *The Gospel According to John.* New York: Crossroad, 1975.

Schwalbe, L.A., and R.N. Rogers. "Physics and Chemistry of the Shroud of Turin: A Summary of the 1978 Investigation." *Analytica Chimica Acta*, vol. 135 (1982): 3–49.

Wilson, Ian. *The Shroud of Turin.* New York: Doubleday and Co., Inc., 1978.